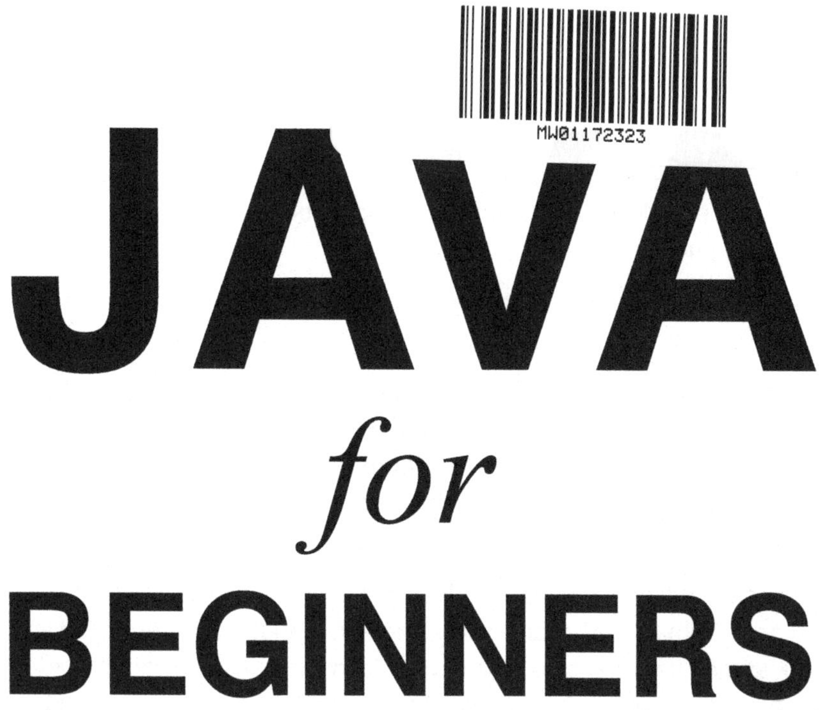

Build Your Dream Tech Career with Engaging Lessons and Projects

SWIFT LEARNING PUBLICATIONS

First Edition

Preface

Welcome to "Java for Beginners," a book designed to be your compass on the exciting journey to becoming a software engineer in the 21st century. Whether you're contemplating enrolling in boot camps or other preparatory programs for your dream tech career or simply exploring the vast world of coding independently, this book is your ideal starting point.

In our rapidly evolving digital landscape, where computer technology and artificial intelligence, such as Chat GPT, continue to shape the future, career choices are being reshaped by the day. "Java for Beginners" aims to empower you with the foundational knowledge needed to thrive in this dynamic environment.

No prior coding experience? No problem! This book adopts a user-friendly approach, using simple language to unravel complex topics. Following the wisdom of the Chinese proverb, "I hear, I forget; I see, I remember; I do, I understand," we've packed this book with hands-on exercises to help you grasp coding vocabulary, master object-oriented programming concepts, navigate file handling techniques, and even explore the application of Chat GPT in coding.

Unlike traditional Java coding books, we have woven in inspiring success stories of self-taught software engineers who have forged their paths to success. So, as you delve into the pages of this book, we invite you to enjoy the journey of discovery and hope that you will find the information both enlightening and practical for your aspiring tech career. Happy coding!

Table of Contents

Introduction

Meet Teddy Smith, a successful self-taught Java developer. Teddy's journey began with JavaScript before delving into Java, where he honed his skills through dedicated practice. Starting from scratch, Teddy developed his programming acumen, eventually landing positions at esteemed companies like JPMorgan & Chase Co., Imagine Software, and Extra Nerds. His advice? Whether you start with Java or JavaScript, the key is to dive in and start learning.

Inspired by Teddy's story, we're reminded of Bill Gates, the iconic figure who revolutionized the world of computing. Dropping out of school at a young age, Gates immersed himself in coding, spending countless hours with friends exploring the intricacies of the Beginner's All-purpose Symbolic Instruction Code (BASIC). Gates' passion for programming manifested early on as he created his first program - a tic-tac-toe game. Through relentless dedication and innovation, Gates went on to become a billionaire, philanthropist, and co-founder of Microsoft, leaving an indelible mark on our world.

And then there's Daphne Koller, the visionary behind Coursera - an online platform offering curated courses from top institutions. A self-taught developer since childhood, Daphne's journey led her to become a Stanford University computer science professor and a MacArthur Fellowship recipient. With a fervent belief in the power of online education and programming, Daphne continues to advocate for accessible learning opportunities for all.

Challenges Beginners Face

While success stories like those of Teddy Smith, Bill Gates, and Daphne Koller inspire us, many beginners struggle with daunting concepts like object-oriented programming, data structures, and algorithms. These topics can feel overwhelming, especially when resources and courses assume prior knowledge or use technical language that's hard to grasp.

Theoretical knowledge is crucial, but it's tough to fully understand concepts without practical application. Beginners often find it challenging to strike the right balance between theory and practice. Learning a concept is one thing, but knowing how to apply it to solve problems or create something meaningful is another. This lack of practical experience can slow down learning and dampen motivation.

Navigating the vast landscape of programming languages, frameworks, and libraries can also leave beginners feeling lost. You need clear guidance on which language to start with, which concepts to focus on, and how to gradually enhance your coding skills.

While there are plenty of resources for beginners, many don't offer a clear path beyond the basics. Once you've mastered the fundamentals, you may find yourself unsure of how to progress further.

Additionally, many Java learning resources use complex language that can confuse beginners. What you really need are resources that simplify these complex concepts, making them easier to understand. Unfortunately, some resources only add to the confusion, leaving you frustrated and disinterested in learning.

But fear not! You're looking for a guide that makes learning Java feel more like an enjoyable journey than a tedious lecture, and that's exactly what this book aims to provide.

Is this Book for You?

This book is geared towards readers aged 16 and up. Whether you're a student on a tight budget, a working professional considering a career change, or someone eager to enhance their skills, this book is for you. It's also relevant for non-technical startup founders or business individuals seeking a basic understanding of Java.

If you're looking to improve your skills for personal satisfaction or to advance your career, you've come to the right place. Even if you aim to impress potential employers or gain a deeper understanding of Java to better oversee a team or project, this book will prove beneficial.

Beginner programmers, educators in computer science or programming, tech enthusiasts, and self-learners alike will find value in this book. Whether you're in high school, college, or an adult seeking a career shift or skill upgrade, this book is your go-to resource.

Whether your goal is to embark on a lucrative career change, create your own app, or simply explore the world of programming out of curiosity, this comprehensive and easy-to-follow guide to learning Java is tailor-made for you.

Benefits of Reading this Book

This book is designed with extensive step-by-step tutorials, examples, exercises, and explanations to guide you through learning core Java concepts. It starts from the basics and gradually progresses to advanced topics, ensuring you gain a comprehensive understanding of Java. The inclusion of exercises and additional resources will give you a head start on your journey towards a career as a programmer.

What sets this book apart is its career-focused approach, tailored specifically for individuals like you who are interested in pursuing a career in programming. This approach will equip you with the skills and knowledge sought after by employers, preparing you well for internships and job opportunities in the tech industry.

The book offers an engaging, interactive, and progressively challenging learning experience. It not only teaches you Java but also introduces you to real-world applications and advanced topics typically not covered in beginner books. You'll explore various exercises and techniques that help explain different Java concepts, including variables and data types, methods, objects, classes, arrays and collections, error handling, operator usage, and program flow control.

By the end of this guide, you'll have acquired fundamental coding skills in Java, empowering you to confidently embark on your own Java projects and potentially secure a job in Java programming or excel in your current roles. Additionally, you'll lay a solid foundation to delve into more complex aspects of Java or even explore other programming languages.

You'll emerge from this guide with a range of skills, including a solid understanding of basic programming concepts, proficiency in object-oriented programming, and the ability to create Java projects. You'll also discover supplementary resources to further your knowledge and explore career opportunities in programming.

Furthermore, the insights shared in this book are not mere overnight wisdom but the culmination of several years of learning, practice, teaching, and refinement. With over 30 years of experience, I bring industry expertise and condensed knowledge to this book, making it easier for you to learn Java effectively.

Testimonials

With the knowledge gained from this book and without any prior programming experience, you can embark on the path to becoming a successful professional programmer. Many self-taught developers have achieved great success in their careers by learning programming on their own and landing their first coding jobs, eventually becoming exceptional software engineers.

Michael "Monty" Widenius, a true coding enthusiast, left Helsinki University of Technology at just 19 years old to pursue a full-time job. Fourteen years later, after dedicated work on his own, he released MySQL, the world's most widely used open-source database.[1] Even at 55, Monty continues to work at his company, serving as an inspiration for aspiring programmers everywhere.

Monty's journey involved sacrificing time spent socializing to focus on programming at home. He devoted several hours each day to learning about computers and the BASIC programming language. Despite lacking prior programming experience, Monty's passion for coding drove him to become a renowned programmer worldwide. He encourages beginner programmers like you to engage with open-source communities and dedicate ample time to personal programming projects.

You can also draw inspiration from Sergei Garcia[2], a front-end developer who kickstarted his career without a computer science degree. Other developers who serve as sources of motivation include Nnenna Ndukwe[3], Julia Evans[4], Colby Williams[5], Cristina Veale[6], many more.

End Results You Can Expect from Reading this Book

Once you've completed this book and practiced all the exercises, you'll no longer feel confused or intimidated by Java. Instead, you'll have the confidence to create your own programs and may even pursue professional opportunities in a tech company. By joining a community of programmers, you'll continue to learn and grow in your new career path.

Reading this book will establish a strong foundation for further exploration of Java, propelling your career forward. You'll become acquainted with one of the world's leading programming languages and may even consider expanding your coding expertise into other languages.

Why You Can Trust Us to Guide You

My journey into the world of technology and mathematics began with a profound appreciation for their intersection. This fascination led me to pursue degrees in these fields at The University of Texas, Austin. After completing my studies, I embarked on a rewarding career as a mathematics and computer applications teacher. Beyond just teaching, I aimed to inspire and guide my students towards their career aspirations.

Throughout my 30+ years in education, I've dedicated myself to understanding the unique needs of my students and advocating for them. I've shared my experiences and insights to positively impact their academic journeys. Over the past 15 years, I've expanded my reach by offering guidance and career counseling to students of all ages. My goal has always been to help them discover their strengths and passions, regardless of gender or socioeconomic background. I take pride in connecting them with career paths that align with their dreams.

With decades of experience as an educator, I've honed my skills to address the diverse needs of students. The guidance and support offered in this book are tailored to ignite your interest in Java programming and set you on the path to a successful career in software development.

It's worth acknowledging that during my own learning journey, the valuable insights and information shared in this book were not readily available. By choosing to explore this book, you're making a wise decision. It's crafted with your needs and concerns in mind, providing practical solutions to the challenges you may face. Consider it your roadmap to mastering Java, step by step.

Chapter Structure

Each chapter in “Java for Beginners: Build Your Dream Tech Career with Engaging Lessons and projects” follows the same structure format to facilitate your learning comfort :

Provides an introductory overview of the chapter’s topic and its relevance to Java programming followed by:

- Explanations: Offers clear and logical explanations of key concepts and principles related to Java programming.
- Examples: Presents helpful examples to illustrate the application of concepts discussed in the chapter.
- Exercises: Includes engaging and fun exercises to reinforce your understanding of the material and provide hands-on practice.
- Sample Answers: Provides sample answers to the exercises along with detailed explanations to aid comprehension.

This User-Friendly book is designed with beginners in mind, offering clear explanations, well-organized content, and plenty of coding exercises to facilitate a hands-on learning experience (learning by doing approach).

Complimentary Introductory Tutoring Session: You’ll receive a free introductory tutoring session to help address any questions or concerns you may have. Visit www.dr-anne.net for more information.

Continued Tutoring Sessions: If you find the introductory session helpful and wish to continue receiving tutoring, additional sessions are available through the author’s website, www.dr-anne.net.

With this structured approach, “Java for Beginners” aims to make learning Java programming accessible, engaging, and effective for readers of all levels.

Chapter 1: Is Java Still Cool For Beginners?

Java has been around since 1995, which might make you wonder if it's still cool to learn today, especially if you're just starting your coding journey. If you're a teenager or an adult curious about programming, this chapter is for you. Here, we'll dive into why Java is an awesome choice for beginners aged 16 and up. We'll take a fun look at Java's journey from its birth to its role in today's tech world, compare it to the trendy JavaScript, and highlight why it's a super useful language to learn. Plus, you'll get some cool tips on how to start coding in Java, making it not just a learning journey but an adventure. So, let's discover together why Java still rocks and how it can open up a world of possibilities for you!

1.1 Exploring Computer Systems for Young Coders

Think of a computer system as a super smart digital buddy that can do tons of cool stuff like typing up your homework, playing games, keeping track of your photos, and a whole lot more. To bring all these awesome tasks to life, computer systems rely on programs created by coders (maybe like you soon!). These systems are a mix of physical parts (hardware) and the programs that run them (software).

1.1.1 Hardware: The Tangible Tech

The hardware is like the body of your computer, including the brain of the operation, the Central Processing Unit (CPU), which does all the thinking. Then you've got the storage spaces for your files and games, the main memory where all the active stuff happens, and the tools you use to interact with your computer, like the keyboard and mouse.

1.1.2 Main Memory: The Brain's Notebook

Main memory, or Random Access Memory (RAM), is where your computer keeps track of what it's currently working on. Think of it as the computer's short-term memory, holding onto your open apps and data. But, like a dream forgotten after waking, everything in RAM disappears when the computer turns off.

1.1.3 Secondary Storage & I/O Devices: Long-term Memory and Communication

Secondary storage is your computer's long-term memory, storing all your files and programs. And then there are I/O (Input/Output) devices. Input devices, like your keyboard and mouse, let you tell the computer what you want to do. Output devices, like your screen and printer, show you what the computer has done.

1.1.4 Software: The Computer's Mind

Software is the soul of your computer, bringing the hardware to life. There are two main:

1.1.4a Operating Systems: The Boss

Operating systems are like the managers of your computer, organizing how you interact with it. Some let you do one thing at a time, while others let you multitask like a pro.

1.1.4b Application Software: The Tools

These are the programs that let you do specific tasks, like writing papers, crunching numbers, playing games, or editing photos.

1.1.4c Programming Languages: The Coder's Language

Programming languages are how you chat with your computer, telling it what to do. They range from super basic machine languages (just 0s and 1s) to high-level languages like Java and JavaScript, which are more like human languages.

In essence, programming languages let you write the instructions that get your computer to do cool stuff, from showing a web page to playing a video game. And with these languages, you'll learn to create algorithms - step-by-step plans for solving problems or performing tasks on your computer. Welcome to the world of coding, where you're the boss, telling your computer exactly what to do to make magic happen!

1.2 Exploring Java: Your Gateway to Programming

Java is like the Swiss Army knife of programming languages - versatile, powerful, and essential for aspiring coders like you. At its heart, Java is an object-oriented language that brings your software ideas to life, from dynamic web applications to mobile apps. It's a language that talks to machines, making it a solid foundation for anyone looking to dive into coding.

What makes Java stand out? It's two things in one: a comprehensive platform equipped with its own toolkit and runtime environment (JRE) and a globally beloved programming language. Thanks to the Java Virtual Machine (JVM), your Java creations can run on any device, whether it's powered by Windows, macOS, Linux, or Solaris. This "write once, run anywhere" capability ensures your Java projects can travel across platforms without a hitch.

Java's structure includes a compiler, the JVM, a rich set of programming tools, and essential libraries, all defined by a specific set of rules and specifications. Despite its age, Java remains the go-to language for beginners, renowned for its user-friendly approach to coding. It marries the simplicity of being both compiled and interpreted: your code is first transformed into a universal bytecode, which is then turned into machine code by the JVM on whatever device you choose.

One of Java's biggest perks for newcomers like you is its minimal dependencies - write your code, compile it into bytecode, and watch it run seamlessly on any Java-friendly platform, no recompilation needed. Its robustness and simplicity have made it the backbone of countless enterprise-level applications.

If you've dabbled in C or C++, you'll find Java's syntax familiar yet simpler, designed for ease of writing, compiling, and debugging. It encourages the development of reusable and modular code, making your programming journey efficient and enjoyable.

To stay ahead of the curve, Oracle regularly updates Java, rolling out new versions every few months to enhance security, fix bugs, and add features. While standard versions get six months of support, Long-Term Maintenance (LTM) versions, like the current Java 17, are supported for around two years, ensuring your Java skills remain fresh and in-demand.

Dive into Java, and you're not just learning a programming language - you're unlocking a world of possibilities in software development, armed with a tool that evolves with technology.

1.3 The Journey of Java: From Inception to Global Impact

The story of Java begins with a spark of innovation at Sun Microsystems in 1991, led by James Gosling along with Patrick Naughton and Mike Sheridan.

This trio, known as the Green Team, crafted Java into a reality. By 1996, Java 1.0 was launched into the public domain, revolutionizing how we interact with digital platforms by offering free runtimes across popular operating systems.[7] Arthur Van Hoff played a key role in reshaping the Java 1.0 compiler, setting the stage for Java's evolution with Java 2 and subsequent versions, each tailored for a variety of platforms.[8]

Java's journey toward standardization in 1997 showcased its potential to meet ISO standards, though Sun Microsystems later retracted from formalizing it, preferring to keep most of Java's implementations accessible at no cost while monetizing specialized products through licensing. In a significant move towards openness, Sun Microsystems released much of Java's core as open-source software in 2006, with its entire foundational code becoming openly available in 2007. Oracle Corporation's acquisition of Java marked a new chapter, underlining Java's enduring legacy in the tech world.

James Gosling is often celebrated as the Father of Java, a testament to his pivotal role in its inception. The name "Java" itself, initially coined as OAK, was chosen for its simplicity and distinctiveness, inspired by the Indonesian island renowned for its coffee - a nod to the beverage that fueled the team's creative sessions.

Today, Java's influence is undeniable, powering over 3 billion devices worldwide. Its versatility allows for a broad spectrum of applications: from Android apps and AI innovations to the core systems in banking and retail. Java's applications extend to desktop software like media players and antivirus programs, web applications, cloud computing, and even the burgeoning fields of Big Data and the Internet of Things (IoT). As Java continues to evolve, it remains a cornerstone of modern software development, bridging the past and future of technology.

1.4 The Edge of Java: Navigating a World of Code

In the vast universe of programming languages, Java carves out its niche by being both compiled and interpreted, marrying the strengths of these two approaches. This unique blend allows Java to transform your source code into bytecode, which the Java Virtual Machine (JVM) then executes, making your applications versatile across different operating systems.

The digital age has seen a meteoric rise in mobile app downloads, with Java being the architect behind a significant chunk of Android applications. This surge in app downloads is a testament to Java's enduring relevance as businesses of all sizes leap onto the mobile bandwagon to connect with their audience more intimately. Consequently, Java developers are in high demand, crafting the digital storefronts that bridge businesses with their customers.

1.4.1 Java vs. JavaScript

Despite sharing part of their names, Java and JavaScript are distinct entities, each with its unique domain of application. Java's realm extends to creating versatile, high-performance applications across platforms, from smart devices to backend systems. JavaScript, on the other hand, brings web applications to life, making browsers more interactive. While learning Java provides a solid foundation in object-oriented programming, venturing into JavaScript, alongside Hypertext Markup Language (HTML) and Cascading Style Sheets (CSS), equips you with the full spectrum of web development skills.

1.4.2 Is Java Worth Your Time?

Absolutely. Java stands out not just for being free and open source but also for its compatibility with various platforms, from Linux to Windows. It's a language that encourages code reusability, enhances security, and boasts a robust support community. For beginners, Java offers a gentle learning curve, paving the way to develop everything from mobile apps to complex enterprise systems.

1.4.3 Java's Simplicity and Strength

Java simplifies coding by eliminating complexities like explicit memory allocation and multiple inheritances. Its strong error-checking mechanism during compilation, coupled with features like exception handling and garbage collection, makes Java both simple and robust.

1.4.4 Multithreading Mastery

In today's data-driven world, where processing speed is paramount, Java's multithreading capabilities allow for efficient Central Processing Unit (CPU) utilization, enabling applications to perform multiple tasks simultaneously. This makes Java an indispensable tool in developing applications that require high interactivity and responsiveness.

1.4.5 Object-Oriented Programming (OOP)

Java's OOP model simplifies software design and development by organizing programs around objects rather than functions. This approach not only enhances code reusability and data security but also aligns closely with real-world problem-solving techniques.

1.4.6 Security, Portability, and Beyond

Java's architecture-neutral bytecode can run anywhere, making it a portable and secure choice for developers. Its "write once, run anywhere" (WORA) capability ensures that Java applications are versatile and adaptable across different environments.

1.4.7 A Thriving Legacy

Java's journey from its inception to becoming a cornerstone of modern software development is a testament to its resilience and adaptability. Its consistent updates and widespread adoption underscore its significance in a rapidly evolving digital landscape.

1.4.8 Why Java Continues to Shine

From its robust performance and dynamic nature to its pivotal role in distributed systems, Java's features make it a preferred language for developers and enterprises alike. Its ability to keep pace with technological advancements and cater to a broad spectrum of applications cements its place as a valuable skill for aspiring programmers.

Embarking on your Java learning journey opens up a world of possibilities, empowering you to build impactful, high-performance applications that drive the digital economy. Whether you're crafting the next hit mobile app or developing complex enterprise solutions, Java offers the tools, community, and versatility to bring your ideas to life.

1.5 Java: The Gateway to Programming for Newcomers

Java stands out as a friendly starting point for anyone diving into the world of programming, not just because it's straightforward to grasp, but also because it's highly sought after, ranking as the fifth most beloved language globally.[9] It's the go-to choice for industry giants like Amazon, Instagram, Microsoft, and Airbnb, thanks to its robust features.

For those keen on mobile app development, Java is the powerhouse behind popular Android applications such as CashApp, Spotify, and Twitter. What makes Java even more appealing to beginners is its vast, supportive community. Whether you're browsing JCP.org[10], Oracle's[11] developer forums, or the myriad of Java questions on Stack Overflow[12], you'll find there's always someone ready to lend a hand or offer insights.

Echoing the sentiments of tech visionaries like Steve Jobs and Bill Gates, learning to code, especially in Java, is more than acquiring a technical skill - it's about nurturing a problem-solving mindset. Programming in Java sharpens your ability to think logically, enhancing your creativity, critical thinking, and analytical prowess. These skills transcend coding, offering valuable insights into solving everyday challenges.

The beauty of Java lies in its accessibility. You don't need a background in mathematics or any prior coding experience to get started. With a commitment to learning, a curious mind, and a readiness to practice and learn from mistakes, you're well on your way. Java not only paves the path to mastering programming concepts but also opens doors to exciting career opportunities.

So, if you're curious about coding and eager to embark on a rewarding journey, Java is your perfect starting point. It's more than a programming language; it's a stepping stone to thinking more innovatively and solving problems more effectively in every aspect of life.

1.6 Career Opportunities in Java

Diving into Java programming opens up a world of career possibilities, from exciting entry-level positions to esteemed senior roles. Enlyft highlights that over 448,975 companies[13] worldwide rely on Java for its unparalleled compatibility, reliability, and user-friendly nature. Renowned organizations such as IBM, Microsoft, Amazon, and Oracle, to name a few, are on a constant lookout for skilled Java developers.

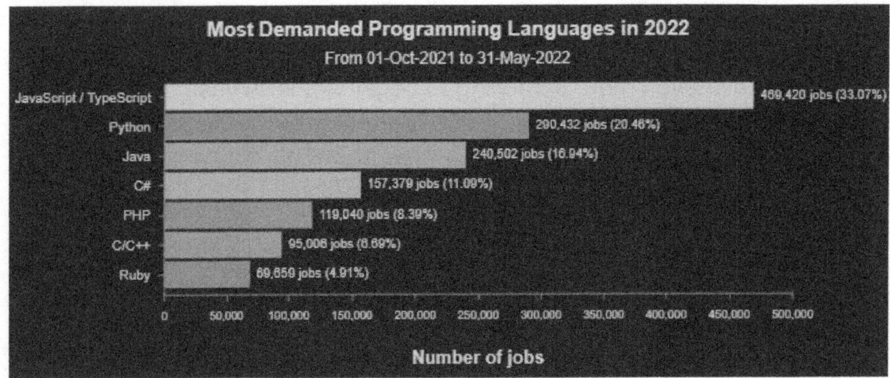

Most Demanded programming Languages in 2022[14]

As an aspiring Java developer, mastering skills like enterprise Java Beans, servlet technology, Java web services, and the J2EE framework will significantly boost your employability. These competencies can land you roles in diverse fields such as:

- Network design and implementation,
- Web development using Java Beans and servlets,
- Software architecture and design,
- Budget planning for tech projects,
- Effective presentation of technical information,
- Project management focusing on tech projects, and
- Specialized web programming.

The journey of a Java developer is not just about the exciting work but also about the rewards that come with it. Salaries for Java developers are impressive, ranging from $92K to over $135K annually (Java Developer Salaries[15]) depending on your experience, role, and location. This range underscores the lucrative nature of a career in Java development.

Armed with the knowledge of Java's enduring relevance and the multitude of opportunities it brings, the next chapter will guide you through the essentials to kickstart your Java journey. Whether you're aiming for your first coding job or looking to scale up in your tech career, Java offers a solid foundation to build upon.

Chapter 2: Kickstarting Your Java Journey

Embarking on your Java programming adventure is an exciting step towards mastering one of the most versatile programming languages out there. This chapter is your guide to installing Java, grasping the basic syntax, and launching your very first Java project. By the end, you'll craft a simple program, proving Java's approachability and your emerging coding prowess.

2.1 Navigating the Java Universe

Imagine a bustling city where myriad organizations, bustling communities, and innovative minds converge to sculpt and evolve Java's landscape. This collaborative and dynamic milieu forms the essence of the Java ecosystem, a realm brimming with JVMs, treasure troves of libraries, a toolkit of development aids, and Integrated Development Environments (IDEs).

2.1.1 Crafting Your Java Workspace

Your journey into Java development begins with setting up a conducive environment, which includes the Java Development Kit (JDK), a friendly IDE, and a simple text editor for code dabbling. Let's unpack these essentials:

2.1.1.1 The Java Development Kit (JDK)

At the core of Java programming is the JDK, your all-access pass to crafting Java applications. It's a comprehensive package that arms you with libraries, a compiler, and the tools necessary to breathe life into your Java creations.

Distinguishing between the JDK, Java Runtime Environment (JRE), and JVM is crucial. The JDK is your creative suite, the JRE is your program's runtime residence, and the JVM is the magic carpet that carries your Java programs across diverse devices.

Remember, the JDK is your toolbox for building Java applications, incorporating the JRE for running those applications and a compiler to translate your Java code into a universal bytecode.

The Compiler's Tale

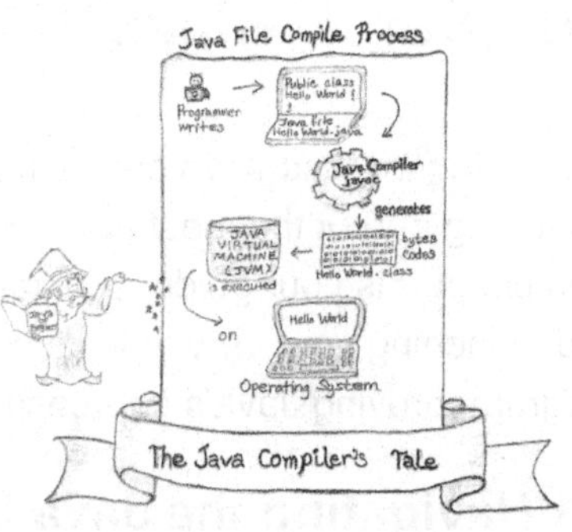

Within the JDK lies the Java compiler, a wizard that transforms your Java scripts into executable bytecode. Soon, we'll guide you through downloading the JDK, setting it up, and meeting your first compiler.

Selecting Your JDK Version

Embarking on this setup journey involves choosing a JDK version. Whether it's Java 11, Java 8, or the robust Java 17, select the one that sings to your coding aspirations. Download it from reputable sources like OpenJDK or Oracle, depending on your requirements for cloud-native or enterprise tools.

For our learning expedition, a standard JDK suffices, especially with its servlet APIs that cater to our web application needs.

2.1.1.2 Downloading Java SE JDK

We'll lean towards the Java SE SDK for its foundational technologies and classes. Oracle's website is your gateway to this essential download, offering various JDK packages. Opt for the Java SE JDK that matches your learning goals.

2.1.1.3 Installing the JDK

Whether you're manually setting up or using an installer, the process is straightforward. Windows and Mac users can benefit from dedicated installers that ease this initial step, incorporating essential components like the JDK proper, Source Code, and the Public JRE for a comprehensive setup.

Command-Line Allies: 'Javac' and 'Java'

With the JDK in place, you unlock the 'javac' command, your compiler's call to action, and the 'java' command, which breathes life into your compiled programs. Test your installation by checking your Java version via the command line. Some IDEs come equipped with a built-in Java compiler, offering a seamless transition into Java development.

As we advance, you'll discover how IDEs and text editors become integral allies in your Java adventure, each enhancing your coding journey with their unique capabilities.

Embark on this chapter with enthusiasm, as it's the foundation of your journey into Java programming - a world where creativity meets logic, and ideas transform into digital reality.

2.2 Jumping into Java with an IDE

Think of an IDE as your all-in-one workspace for crafting Java applications. It's much like a swiss army knife for coding, packing everything you need into a single, user-friendly platform. This includes a text editor to type your code, a file manager to keep your projects organized, and special tools that help you format, test, and run your Java programs with ease.

2.2.1 Popular Java IDEs for Beginners

For those just starting with Java, there are several beginner-friendly IDEs such as IntelliJ, Eclipse, NetBeans, and Visual Studio Code (VS Code). These IDEs work great on Ubuntu/Linux, Mac OS, and Windows, ensuring you can code comfortably on your preferred operating system.

2.2.2 What's Inside an IDE?

- Code Editor: Makes writing and editing your code a breeze.
- Compiler: Transforms your written code into a language your computer understands.
- Debugger: Lets you hunt down and fix any bugs or mistakes in your code.
- Automated Tools: Save you time by handling repetitive tasks, like setting up a user interface.
- Profilers: Help make your code run faster and more efficiently as it grows.

Some IDEs even offer:

- Object and Class Browsers: Let you inspect and navigate through your code's structure.
- Version Control: Keeps track of your code changes, allowing you to undo mistakes by reverting to earlier versions.

2.2.3 Why Use an IDE?

- All-in-One: Access all your coding tools in one spot.
- Smart Coding Assistance: Get suggestions and corrections as you type.
- Fast Development: Streamline your coding process from start to finish.

- Learning As You Code: Continuous feedback helps you learn and improve.

2.2.4 Choosing the Right IDE

IDEs come in different flavors, each catering to various coding needs and preferences. Whether you're developing for mobile, web, or desktop, there's an IDE out there for you. Some IDEs specialize in specific languages, while others are versatile, supporting multiple programming languages:

- Mobile Development: Look into Titanium Mobile or PhoneGap.
- Cloud-Based Development: Explore cloud IDEs like Nitrous or Cloud9 for flexibility.
- Specific to Microsoft or Apple: Try out Visual Studio or Xcode.
- HTML Development: DreamWeaver and FrontPage are go-tos for website creation.

2.2.5 Security Within IDEs

While IDEs are fantastic for development, integrating security testing into them can be challenging. The best approach is to choose IDEs that support security plugins or extensions, ensuring your applications are safe and secure right from the development phase.

2.2.6 Getting Started

Diving into Java programming with an IDE is like setting off on an adventure with the best tools at your disposal. Choose an IDE that resonates with your project needs and personal coding style, and you'll find Java programming a rewarding and enjoyable journey.

2.3 Getting Started with Text Editors for Java Programming

Text editors are your first step into the world of Java programming. They're simple tools that let you type up and tweak your Java code as plain text. While some are basic with minimal styling options, others are more advanced, specifically tailored for coding.

Simple Text Editors

For beginners, starting with a straightforward text editor is a great choice. It allows you to focus on learning Java without any distractions. Tools like TextEdit on Mac, Notepad on Windows, and GEdit for Ubuntu are perfect for dipping your toes into coding.

Programming Text Editors: A Step Up

As you grow more comfortable with Java, you might crave tools designed with coding in mind. These programming text editors are a step up, offering features that make coding smoother and more efficient. These features include:

- Auto-Indentation: Keeps your code neat and readable.
- Syntax Highlighting: Colors different parts of your code, making it easier to read and spot errors. Imagine comments in green, keywords in blue, making your code look like a vibrant map that's easy to navigate.
- Built-in Compilation and Execution: Some editors allow you to compile and run your code right there, eliminating the need to switch between your editor and the command line.

Examples of programming text editors are JEdit, which works across Mac, Windows, and Ubuntu, and TextPad for Windows users.

Choosing the Right Text Editor for You

If you're just starting with Java and prefer not to get bogged down with complex IDE features, a programming text editor might be your best bet. For a seamless experience where you don't have to jump between your editor and the terminal to compile and run your code, consider using NetBeans.

Initially, focus solely on writing and executing your Java code in NetBeans. This approach allows you to gradually familiarize yourself with more complex aspects of programming without feeling overwhelmed. As you progress, you'll naturally start exploring and utilizing the more advanced features of your text editor.

2.3.1 Your First Steps into Java Programming

Choosing the right text editor is like picking the perfect backpack for an adventure; it should have just the right features to support you as you embark on your Java programming journey. Start simple, grow your skills, and before you know it, you'll be exploring the vast landscape of Java with confidence and curiosity.

2.4 Setting Up Your Java Development Workspace

Embarking on your Java programming journey means setting up a space where you can freely code, compile, and run your Java applications. Think of it as setting up a studio for your creative projects, where everything you need is within reach. Here's how to get your Java development environment ready, focusing on using Apache NetBeans, a friendly IDE that simplifies Java coding for beginners.

Step 1: Installing the Java Development Kit (JDK)

Before diving into coding, you need the right tools. The Java Development Kit (JDK) is your first companion, providing you with the essential utilities to write Java applications.

1. Check Your Windows Version: Press `Win + I`, click on `System`, and then About to find out if your system is 32-bit or 64-bit.
2. Download JDK: Visit the Oracle website[16] and choose the JDK version that matches your system (either 32-bit or 64-bit). Oracle regularly updates Java, so go for the latest version to enjoy new features and better security.
3. Install JDK: Run the installer you downloaded. Follow the prompts, and remember the folder where you installed JDK - you'll need this path later.

Step 2: Setting Up Environment Variables

To make Java commands accessible from anywhere on your system, adjust the environment variables as follows:

Setting Up `JAVA_HOME`: This variable points to where JDK is installed, helping other programs find your JDK installation.

- Press `Win + S`, type `env`, and click on `Edit the system environment variables`.
- In the `System Properties` window, click `Environment Variables`.
- Under `System Variables`, click `New`, and enter `JAVA_HOME` as the variable name and the path to your JDK installation as the variable value.

Updating the `Path` Variable: This ensures your system recognizes Java commands.

- Find the `Path` variable under `System Variables` and click `Edit`.
- Click `New` and add `%JAVA_HOME%\bin`. This directs your system to use the JDK's tools.

Step 3: Installing Apache NetBeans

Apache NetBeans provides a user-friendly interface to code, compile, and run Java applications. It's perfect for beginners due to its intuitive setup and comprehensive features.

4. Download Apache NetBeans: Visit the NetBeans[17] website and download the installer suitable for your system. Please see 2.4.2 "Download and Install and IDE" for detailed instructions on how to download and install IDE Netbeans.

5. Install Apache NetBeans: Run the installer and follow the on-screen instructions. NetBeans automatically detects your JDK installation, making the setup smoother.

Verify Your Setup

To ensure everything is set up correctly:

- Open NetBeans, create a new Java project, and try writing a simple program, like printing `"Hello, World!"` to the console.
- Run your program within NetBeans. If you see `"Hello, World!"` in the output, congratulations! Your Java development environment is ready.

2.4.1 Your Creative Studio for Java

Setting up your Java development environment is like preparing a canvas for painting. With Apache NetBeans and JDK in place, you're equipped with the best tools to start coding. Remember, the journey of a thousand lines of code begins with a single setup. Happy coding!

2.4.2 Download and Install an IDE

We install the IDE last because it depends on a properly configured development environment to search and find the JDK tools - the ***javac*** command (Java Compiler) to compile your code and the ***java*** command (the JVM) to execute the compiled code.

For a smoother coding experience, it's highly recommended to use an IDE. An IDE offers an advanced text editor with various helpful features for coding. In addition, it includes a user-friendly graphical interface for debugging, compiling, and executing your applications. These integrated features are designed to assist coding and enhance your learning process. The IDE introduced in this book is NetBeans, developed by Apache.

To download NetBeans, type this URL in the web address bar:
http://netbeans.apache.org/download/index.html
Click on the download button for the latest version of the NetBeans. NetBeans updates and releases a new version four times a year.

After clicking on the download button, look for the bullet pointed "Installers" and select the correct installer for your operating system:

- Binaries (Platform Independent): netbeans -18-bin.zip (SHA-512, PGP ASC) version 18
- Installers:
  - ☐ Apache-NetBeans-18-bin-windows-x64.exe (SHA-512, PGP ASC) ; Windows
  - ☐ Apache-NetBeans-18-bin-linux-x64.sh (SHA-512, PGP ASC) ; Linux
  - ☐ Apache-NetBeans-18-bin-macosx.dmg (SHA-512, PGP ASC) ; Mac OS
- Source: netbeans-18-source.zip (SHA-512, PGP ASC)

If you find yourself on a different page, don't worry. Just click on the first link we have given you to download NetBeans from the website we recommend. After it is downloaded, simply double-click on the installer to finish installing it. Once this is done, you'll be ready to start writing your very first Java program. It is that easy!

2.4.3 Check Your Understanding

1. **What is a text editor?**
    a. An editor that resembles a code editor, for changing code.
    b. An editor that resembles a code editor.
    c. A program that edits text.
    d. A program that edits code in plain text.

2. **Which of the following is a function of most programming text editors?**
    a. Debugging
    b. Executing and highlighting code.
    c. Executing code and controlling a debugger.
    d. Write code on your behalf.

3. **What does the acronym IDE stand for in full?**
    a. Integrated Down Editor
    b. Inside Development Environment
    c. Integrated Development Environment
    d. Integrated Development Editor

4. **What is JDK in full?**
    a. Java Development Kit
    b. Java Data Kit
    c. Java Disintegrated Kit
    d. Java Development Keeper

5. **What is a run-time environment?**
    a. An environment created during program execution, allowing you to track instructions.
    b. An environment created during program execution, allowing the code to track instructions.
    c. An environment created when compiling your program, allowing you to track instructions.
    d. An environment created during program debugging, allowing you to track instructions.

6. **What is an error diagnostic?**
    a. What's entered post error detection.
    b. Information displayed when an error is detected during Java program creation.

c. Any information that interferes with the operation or performance of your Java program.
d. Correction of errors detected in your code.

7. **What is a compiler?**
   a. A program that translates spoken words.
   b. A program that converts your code from plain text to machine readable form.
   c. A program that translates code to a foreign language.
   d. A hardware component of the JDK.

8. **Which of the following are advantages or benefits of IDE?**
   a. Makes code run faster.
   b. Eases coding in Java.
   c. DE is faster.
   d. IDE operates slower than JDK.

9. **Which of the following is an IDE?**
   a. CodeBlocks
   b. Code::Blocks
   c. Code:::Blocks
   d. Code:Blocks

10. **What is JVM in full?**
    a. Java Virtual Machine
    b. Java Verified Machine
    c. Java Version Machine

11. **What is the difference between a text editor and code editor?**
    a. Both editors can edit plain text.
    b. A text editor can edit computer readable language only.
    c. A code editor is designed specifically for writing codes while a text editor isn't.
    d. A text editor has more features and capabilities than a code editor.

12. **What is debugging?**
    a. Removing colors from your code.
    b. Converting your code to a machine readable form.
    c. Scanning for errors in your code for correction.
    d. Removing bugs or errors from your code and development environment.

Answers: 1.c 2.b 3.c 4. 5.a 6.b 7.b 8. b (IDE has special tools that make coding easier and more convenient. However, it doesn't automatically make your code run faster. IDEs are good for things like writing code, fixing errors, and keeping your software projects organized.); 9.b 10.a 11.c (Text editors are like all-purpose tools, while code editors are like tools made just for coding. Code editors have extra features that make coding easier, which regular text editors don't have.); 12.d (Debugging means finding and fixing mistakes or problems in your code so that it works the way you want it to.)

2.5 Crafting Your First Java Adventure: "Hello World!"

Welcome to the thrilling world of Java programming! Your first mission, should you choose to accept it, is to craft the time-honored "Hello World" program. This rite of passage for all budding programmers is your gateway into the realm of Java. Fear not, young coder, for this journey will unravel the mysteries of Java programming in the simplest terms.

You will use the NetBeans (http://netbeans.apache.org/download/index.html) that you installed following the steps in lesson 2.4.2. You will see this icon on your desktop.
Follow the Java Quick Tutorial in the Net Beans website to create your project: https://netbeans.apache.org/tutorial/main/kb/docs/java/quickstart/

Project Setup
Follow these steps to initialize a new Java Project:

1. Within your Integrated Development Environment (IDE), navigate to File > New Project or simply click the "New Project" icon in the toolbar.
2. The "New Project" wizard will appear. Here, choose "Java Application" as depicted in the illustration below. Then, proceed by clicking "Next."

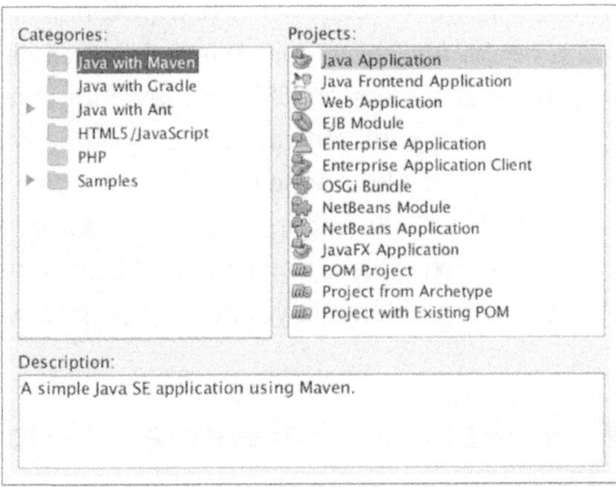

Initializing Name and Location

Upon embarking on your initial Java project setup, you will encounter a prompt to download and activate Java support. Pay close attention to the guidance of the setup wizard and proceed with the recommended installation steps. In the Name and location page of the wizard, enter "Hello World App" into the "Project Name" field as shown below:

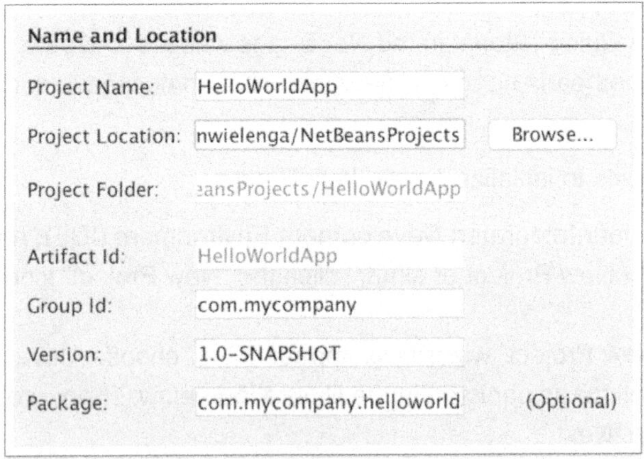

Click "Finish." The project is now created and opened.

Creating a Java Source File

Simply right-click on the package name in your project structure and select "New I Java Class" from the context menu, as illustrated in the following figure:

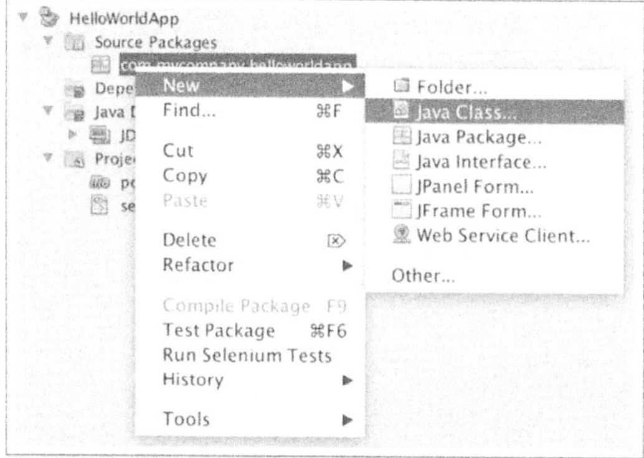

In the new Java Class wizard, type Main in the Class Name field as shown in the figure below:

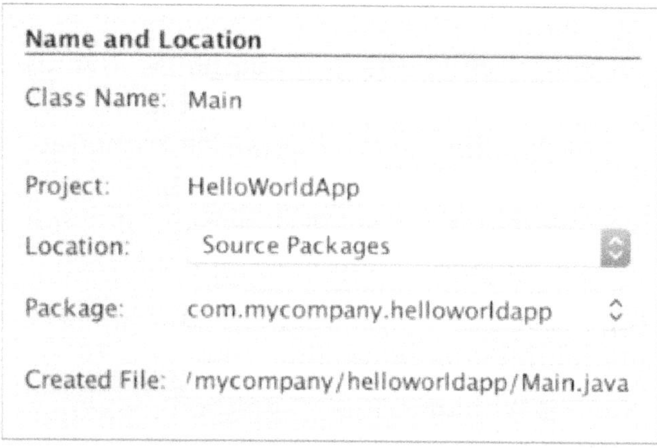

Click "Finish."
Now, the Java source file is created and opened.

Your screen should now display the elements as depicted in the illustration below:

- **Project Window**: Located on the left, this displays a hierarchical view of your project's components, such as source files and libraries that your code relies on.
- **Source Editor**: Occupies the central part of your screen, where you'll spend most of your time coding. Currently, it's displaying a Java source file named Main.
- **Navigator**: Found at the bottom left, this feature is handy for swiftly

moving between elements within the chosen class.

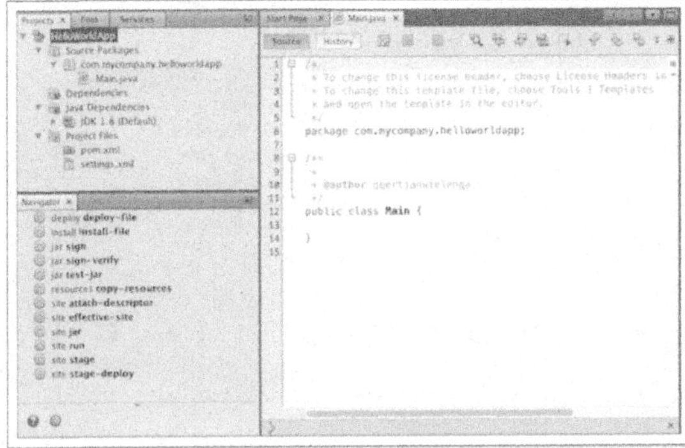

Incorporating Code into Your Java Source File

A skeleton main class has already been created for you. Now, let's add a simple command to output a 'hello world' message. Here is how to proceed:

- Inside the curly brackets, enter `psvm` and hit Tab. This will expand to the full `public static void main` method.
- Within this method, type `sout` and press Tab to automatically generate a `System.out.println` statement.
- Inside the parentheses and quotation marks, input `"hello world."`

After these steps, your code should resemble the following structure:

```
/*
 * To change this license header, choose License Headers in F
 * To change this template file, choose Tools | Templates
 * and open the template in the editor.
 */
package com.mycompany.helloworldapp;

/**
 *
 * @author geertjanwielenga
 */
public class Main {
    public static void main(String[] args) {
        System.out.println("hello world");
    }
}
```

HelloWorldApp-Apache NetBeans IDE 11.0

Observe that pressing Ctrl + Space triggers the editor to display various options for completing the code at the cursor's location, along with corresponding documentation:

For comprehensive details on the features available for code assistance, refer to the "Code Assistance in the NetBeans IDE Java Editor: A Reference Guide."

Running the Application

Make sure the Java source file is saved, then right-click on the project and select "Run," or go to the "Run" menu and choose "Run Project." Next, click "Select Main Class."

In the "Output" window, which can be opened from the "Window" menu, you should see the message:"Congratulations! Your application works."

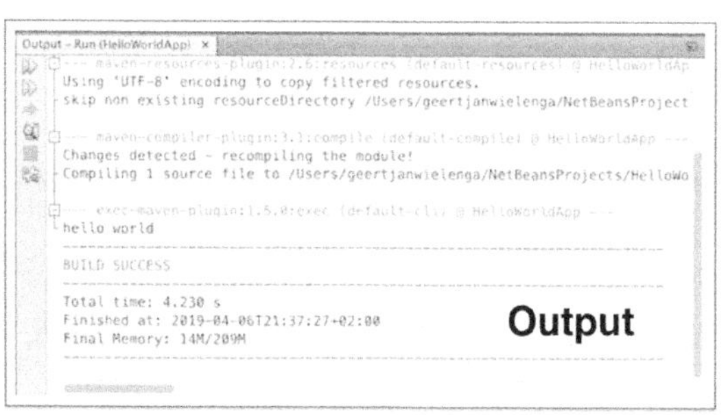

To check the build output, open the "Files" window from the "Window" menu, and look under the "target" node. You've now mastered the basic tasks in Java development. For a comprehensive guide on the full Java development process, including testing and debugging, refer to "Developing General Java Applications."

2.5.1 Let the Adventure Begin

With NetBeans, the coding tool we set up earlier, you're ready to start creating magic with code.

Here's how you summon your first spell:

1. Opening the Gateway: Launch NetBeans and beckon a new project into existence by navigating through `File > New Project.`
2. Choosing Your Path: When faced with the New Project dialog box, align your destiny with `Java With Maven` and `Java Application`. If it's your maiden voyage, you might encounter a message urging you to activate this feature. Fearlessly click `Next` and empower any modules asking for your acknowledgment.
3. Crafting the Spell: In the heart of your project, inscribe the following incantation:

```
public class HelloWorld {
    public static void main(String[ ] args) {
        System.out.println("Hello World!");
        // Hello World! Behold, the birth of communication with
the digital realm!
    }
}
```

Unraveling the "Hello World" Enigma

- Java Classes: Think of `HelloWorld` as your digital fortress. It's where your commands come to life. In Java, every spell (program) begins with a class.
- The Main Method: This is the sacred ground where your code springs into action. The `public static void main(String[] args)` is the portal through which your program steps into reality.
- The Echo of "Hello World": The `System.out.println("Hello World!");` is your first proclamation to the world, a declaration that will echo across the console, announcing your arrival in the coder's realm.
- Java Strings & Comments: Strings are the whispers of your program, encapsulated in quotes, while comments (`//Hello World!`) are the silent observers, guiding future travelers.

2.5.2 Compile Your Code With the JDK

Next, you'll harness the power of the JDK compiler, transforming your written spell into an executable potion known as bytecode.

Summoning the Compiler: Use the `javac HelloWorld.java` command in the console's realm to compile your code into bytecode.

2.5.3 Bringing Your Code to Life

The Incantation: Within the same domain as your `HelloWorld.java`, command `java HelloWorld` to breathe life into your program. Behold the greeting "Hello World!" materializing on your screen.

2.5.4 Create and Add the JAR Tool to Your Existing Classpath

Creating the JAR: This mystical container compresses your code into a single vessel. Use *`jar -create -file intro.jar HelloWorld.class`* to encapsulate your bytecode.

Enchanting the Classpath: With the spell `java -cp intro.jar HelloWorld`, link your JAR to the classpath, summoning the program within.

Congratulations, valiant coder! You've successfully crafted your first Java program, embarking on a journey of endless possibilities. As you venture forth, the arcane syntax and grammar of Java await to further unlock the secrets of this powerful realm.

Chapter 3: Java "Grammar" Rules

Just like most other programming languages, a few rules help when coding in Java. This chapter focuses on basic grammar rules for java you need to pay attention to in terms of syntax, naming conventions, and using comments.

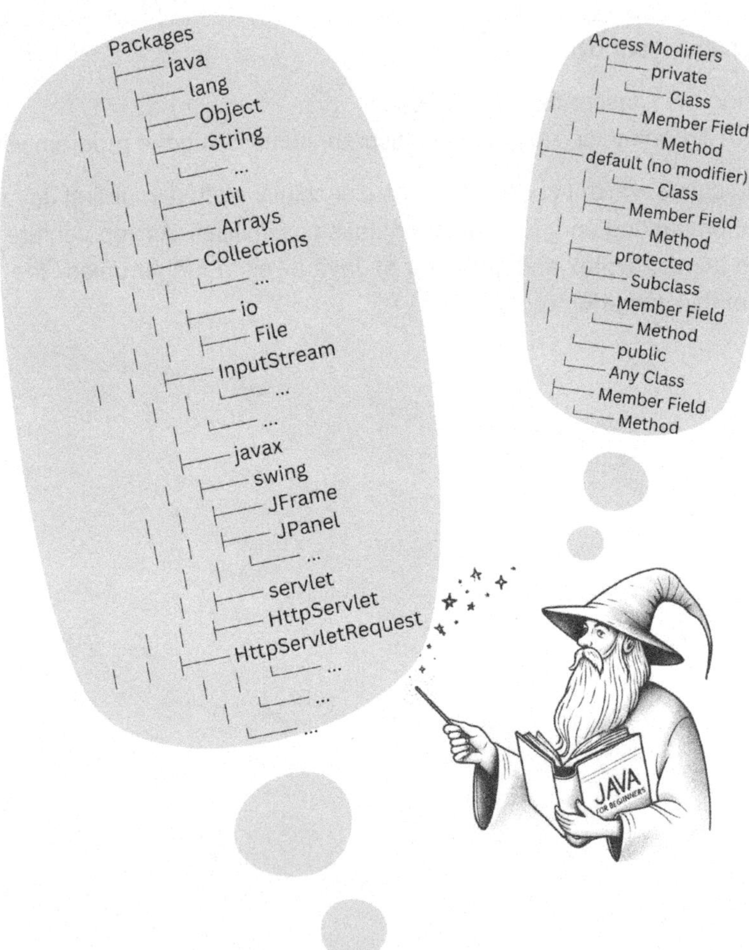

3.1 Naming Classes and Interfaces

When you're learning to program in Java, there are a few basic rules to make your code easy to understand and work with. Remember these rules as you write your Java programs:

1. **Make Your Code Readable**: It's important that your code is easy for others (and yourself) to read and understand. This means writing clearly and following a consistent style.
2. **Look at Examples**: Check out code written by experienced programmers. See how they make their code easy to read and follow.
3. **Naming Convention**: This is about how you name things in your Java code. It helps make your code organized and clear.
   - Variables and Methods: Use 'CamelCase' for naming. This means you start with a lowercase letter and then use uppercase letters to start new words, like `myVariable or calculateTotal`.
   - Classes and Interfaces: Use 'TitleCase' for these. Start each word with an uppercase letter, like `MyClass` or `UserInterfa`ce.
4. **Naming Packages**: Packages are like folders that help organize your code. Package names usually start with a lowercase letter and often include the domain name of your organization in reverse. For example, **com.mycompany.myapp**.

3.1.1 Naming Classes

Classes are like blueprints for objects. You should name them with 'TitleCase', which means you capitalize the first letter of each word. They are usually nouns (names of things). For example:

- `public class Car {}`
- `public class Bicycle {}`
- `public class Student {}`

3.1.2 Naming Interfaces

Interfaces are like contracts for classes, telling them what they can do. They are often adjectives (describing words) but can sometimes be nouns. Like class names, you also capitalize the first letter of each word in interface names. For example:

- `public interface Readable {}`
- `public interface Drawable {}`
- `public interface List {}`

By following these naming rules, you help others (and yourself) understand what each part of your code is supposed to do.

When you're coding in Java, naming methods and variables correctly helps make your code more understandable.

3.1.3 Naming Methods:

Methods are the actions your code can perform, typically beginning with a verb as they "do" something. It's customary to write method names in 'camelCase', where the name starts with a lowercase letter and capitalizes the first letter of each new word. The method name should clearly indicate what the method does, facilitating easy understanding and usage within the codebase.

Examples:

- `public void saveReport(Report report) {}`
- `public void deleteItem(Item item) {}`
- `public int calculateTotal(int number1, int number2) {}`

3.1.4 Naming Variables:

Variables serve as containers for storing data within a program. It's customary to use 'camelCase' when naming variables, where the name starts with a lowercase letter and capitalizes the first letter of each new word. The variable name should be concise yet descriptive, clearly indicating its purpose within the code. In some cases, a single letter may suffice for variable names, such as 'i' often used in loops for iteration purposes.

Examples:

- `int age;`
- `String firstName;`
- `double totalPrice;`
- `for (int i = 0; i < 10; i++) { } // 'i' is a loop counter.`

Remember, good names make your code much easier to read and understand!

When writing Java programs, how you name your variables is important because it helps others understand what your code is doing.

1. **Variable Names Start with Lowercase**: Begin each variable name with a lowercase letter. The name should give a clue about what the variable is used for. Avoid using vague names like 'data' or names

that don't relate to the purpose of the variable, like 'flower' or the names of friends.

2. **Choose Meaningful Names**:
   - Long Names: These can describe the variable's purpose better, but they make your code longer. Example: totalDistanceTravelled.
   - Short Names: They make your code shorter but might not explain much about the variable. Example: dist.

   Compare:
   - Long name: `totalDistance = speed * time;`
   - Short name: `d = s * t;`

3. **Names of Parameters:**
   - Parameters are the values you pass to methods. Their names should be short and clear, sometimes even just a letter.
   - Example: In a method `public boolean isSquare(int sideLength)`, `sideLength` is a parameter.

4. **Names of Local Variables:**
   - Local variables are used inside methods and their names are usually short.
   - They should be declared close to where they are used and their purpose can be explained with a comment.
   - Example: `int count; // counts the number of items`

5. **Fields and Static Variables:**
   - Field (or class) variables are used by the whole class. Their names are longer to help explain their purpose.
   - Since they are used in different parts of the class, you often explain their purpose with comments in the code.

Remember, the name of a variable should help anyone reading your code to understand what the variable is for. This makes your code easier to read and maintain.

Naming of Enums

- Enums in Java are a way to define collections of constants. The concept of using Enums might be introduced to beginners who have already grasped the basics of Java, such as classes, objects, and basic data types.

- Writing enum names in all uppercase letters is a convention that aligns with how constants are named in Java, which is usually covered early in learning Java.
- Example:

```
public enum Direction {
    NORTH, EAST, SOUTH, WEST;
}
```

For beginners, the focus is usually on understanding what Enums and Annotations are and how they are used in Java. The naming conventions, while important, are part of a larger discussion on Java's best practices and coding standards, which can be understood as learners become more comfortable with the language.

When you start learning Java, one of the first things you should learn is how to name your methods, variables, and classes. This is known as 'naming conventions' and helps make your code easy to read and maintain. Here are some basic rules to follow:

1. **Class Names and File Names**: The name of your Java file should match the class name inside it. So, if you have a class named `MyClass`, the file should be named `MyClass.java`.
2. **One Class Per File**: Write each class in its own file, which ends with `.java`. You can organize many of these files into folders known as 'packages'.
3. **Case Sensitivity**: Remember that Java is case-sensitive. It treats uppercase and lowercase letters differently. So, `String` and `string` are not the same.
4. **The Main Method**: Every Java program starts from a 'main method'. This is where your program begins running. The main method looks like this:
   `public static void main(String[ ] args)`.
5. **Class Naming**: When naming your classes, start each word with an uppercase letter. For example, use `MyFirstJavaClass`.
6. **Saving Files**: Save your Java files with the class name followed by **.java**. For example, `MyFirstJavaClass.java`.
7. **Curly Braces**: Curly braces `{}` are used in Java to group code together. This helps organize your code into sections.
8. **End Lines with Semicolons**: In Java, each instruction ends with a semicolon `;`. This tells Java it's the end of a command."

You will learn topics like "function and procedure methods" and the distinction between them in the intermediate level. For beginners, understanding that methods are sets of instructions and focusing on syntax and naming conventions is a great start.

Formatting

When you write Java programs, keeping your code well-formatted is important. Good formatting makes your code easier to read and understand. Here are some basic formatting rules:

1. **Consistent Braces**: Use braces `{}` consistently. This helps show which parts of your code are grouped together.
2. **Line Length**: Try to keep each line of your code short, ideally under 80 characters. This way, you won't have to scroll horizontally to read your code.
3. **Indentation**: Indent your code to show its structure. Indentation is usually 4 spaces. This helps you see which code belongs to which block, like inside a method or an if statement.
4. **Position of Braces**: There are a couple of ways to place your braces:

<table>
<tr>
<td>Option 1: Open brace at the end of a line, close brace on its own line.

<pre>
if (x < y) {
    x = y;
    y = 0;
} else {
    x = 0;
    y = y / 2;
}
</pre></td>
<td>Option 2: Open brace on a new line. Some programmers prefer this, but it takes up more space.

<pre>
if (x < y)
{
    x = y;
    y = 0; }
else
{
    x = 0;
    y = y / 2;
}
</pre></td>
</tr>
</table>

5. **Choosing a Style**: Stick with one style of formatting through your learning. Once you're comfortable, you can try different styles to see

which you prefer.Remember, the key is consistency. Whether you're working alone or with others, having a consistent style makes your code more organized and easier to work with.

Control Flow Structures Using Braces

In Java programming, how you use braces { } and format your code is important. This helps make your code clear and reduces the chance of making mistakes.

Using Braces in Control Flow

- Sometimes, not using braces can lead to bugs (errors in your code).
- For example, if you write **`if (flag) validate( );update( );`**, it might look like both **`validate( )`** and **`update( )`** are part of the **`if`** condition, but actually, only **`validate( )`** is. This can cause errors.
- A better way is to always use braces, like this:

```
if (flag) {
    validate();
    update();
}
```

- Use braces in other structures too, like if-else, while, and for loops.

Formatting Tips

- **Indentation**: Use spaces to indent the inner part of methods, classes, and control structures (like **`if`** statements). This shows the structure of your code.
- **Braces**: You can put the opening brace at the end of a line or on a new line, and always put the closing brace on its own line.
- **Line Length**: Keep each line of your code under 80 characters. If it's longer, break it into multiple lines.
- **Nesting**: Avoid too many levels of nested statements. Try to keep it to two or three levels.
- **Spaces and Blank Lines**: Use spaces around operators (like =, !=, ==) and blank lines to separate sections of code for better readability.

3.1.5 Capitalization Rules

- Start method names, variable names, and package names with lowercase letters. For example, `calculateTotal`.

- Start class names with uppercase letters. If the name has multiple words, capitalize each word. For example, `MyClass`.
- **Example:** `interestRate` **for a variable or method, and** `InterestRate` for a class.

Remember, these formatting rules are not just about making your code look nice, but they also help prevent errors and make your code easier to understand and maintain.

3.1.6 Using Comments

In Java, comments are parts of your code that the computer ignores. They are really useful for explaining what your code does, both to others and to yourself in the future.

Why Use Comments?

- Understanding: They help make your code easier to understand.
- Debugging: You can temporarily stop parts of your code from running by commenting them out. This is helpful when you're testing different parts of your code.
- Readability: Comments can make your code more readable by explaining what a particular part of the code is for.
- Documentation: They provide important information about your methods, variables, and classes.

Types of Comments in Java

1. **Single-line Comments**: Use // at the beginning of a line. Java will ignore everything on that line after //. These are great for short notes or temporary disabling of code.

```
// This is a single-line comment
int number = 10; // This sets the number to 10
```

2. **Multi-line Comments**: Use /* to start and */ to end. Everything between these will be a comment. Good for longer explanations that take up more than one line.

```
/* This is a multi-line comment
   It can span over multiple
   lines of your code */
```

3. **Documentation Comments:** Use /** to start and */ to end. These are used by the **javadoc** tool to create documentation for your code.

```
/**
 * This method calculates the sum of two integers.
 *
 * @param num1 The first integer to add.
 * @param num2 The second integer to add.
 * @return The sum of num1 and num2.
 */
public int add(int num1, int num2) {
    return num1 + num2;
}
```

Single Line Comments in Java

Example of Single-line Comments

```
public class ExampleComment {
    public static void main(String[] args) {
        int i = 15; // The value of the i variable is 15
        System.out.println(i); // Prints the value of i
    }
}
```

Comments are a great way to make your code more understandable, so make sure to use them effectively!

Output

The code in the example uses multi-line comments in Java. Let's break it down:

What Happens in the Code?

- The program prints the number 20.
- It uses multi-line comments to explain or temporarily disable parts of the code.

Multi-line Comments in Java

- To write a comment that spans multiple lines, start with /* and end with */.
- Java ignores everything between these markers.
- This is useful for explaining complex parts of your code or commenting out several lines at once.

Example of Multi-line Comments

```
public class ExampleComment2 {
    public static void main(String[] args) {
        /* You can now declare the variable
           and print it in Java. */
        int i = 20;
        System.out.println(i);

        /* The following lines are commented out:
        float k = 5.9;
        Float l = 3.3;
        System.out.println(k + l);
        */
    }
}
```

- In this example, the part between `/*` and `*/` is a comment. Java doesn't run this part.
- The code prints `20`, but it doesn't run the part where **`k`** and **`l`** are declared and printed because they are inside a multi-line comment.

Using Comments

- Use `/* */` for longer comments or when you want to comment out multiple lines of code.
- Use // for shorter, single-line comments.

Comments are great for making notes in your code or temporarily stopping some parts of your code from running."

Documentation Comment in Java

- As you progress in Java programming, especially in large projects, you'll use documentation comments to create detailed descriptions of your code. This is especially important for APIs (Application Programming Interfaces), which other developers might use.
- Good documentation helps reduce programming time, lowers the chance of errors, and results in fewer bugs.

How to Write Documentation Comments

- Use `/**` to start and `*/` to end a documentation comment.
- Inside these comments, you can include special tags that provide specific types of information.
- The **`javadoc`** tool reads these comments to generate HTML documentation for your code.

Example of a Documentation Comment

```
/**
 * This is an example of a documentation comment.
 * You can use different tags here to describe parameters,
 * the author, version, and more.
 * You can also use HTML tags for formatting.
 */
```

Common Javadoc Tags

- **`@docRoot`**: Shows the path to the root directory of your documentation.
- **`@author`**: Adds the author's name.
- **`@code`**: Displays text as code format.
- **`@version`**: Specifies the version of the code or class.
- **`@since`**: Indicates the release version this code belongs to.
- **`@param`**: Describes parameters for methods.
- **`@return`**: Describes what a method returns.

Why Use These Tags?

- These tags help organize your documentation and make it clear and useful. They show who wrote the code, what each part does, the version, and more. This is very helpful for anyone who uses your code, including yourself in the future.

Remember, good documentation is a key part of professional programming, especially in large projects!

3.1.7 Check Your Understanding

1. Why is CamelCase used for naming methods and variables in Java?
   - A) To indicate a new instance.
   - B) For easier readability and to follow Java conventions.
   - C) Because it's a requirement for Java compilation.
   - D) To differentiate Java code from HTML.

2. True or False: In Java, class names are typically nouns and start with a lowercase letter, while interface names are often adjectives and start with an uppercase letter.
   - True
   - False

3. It is recommended to always use braces {} in control structures for:
    - A) Making the code longer.
    - B) Preventing potential bugs and enhancing code clarity.
    - C) It's a syntax requirement in Java.
    - D) Making the code run faster.
4. The purpose of using comments in Java code is to:
    - A) Increase memory usage.
    - B) Improve the readability and maintainability of the code.
    - C) Make the program run more efficiently.
    - D) Change how the code executes.
5. How do you write a multi-line comment in Java?
    - A) `// Comment here //`
    - B) `<!-- Comment here -->`
    - C) `/* Comment here */`
    - D) `/* Comment here */`
6. True or False: The javadoc tool in Java is used to fix bugs in the code.
    - True
    - False
7. Indentation in Java programming is important because:
    - A) It helps in reducing the size of the code.
    - B) It's mandatory for the code to compile.
    - C) It helps define the structure of the program, making it more readable.
    - D) It increases the execution speed of the program.
8. The recommended maximum length for a line of code in Java is:
    - A) 80 characters, to avoid horizontal scrolling and maintain readability.
    - B) 200 characters, to fit more code on the screen.
    - C) 50 characters, to save memory.
    - D) There is no recommended maximum length.
9. The `@param tag` in a Javadoc comment is used for:
    - A) Marking deprecated methods.
    - B) Describing the parameters of a method.
    - C) Indicating the return type of a method.
    - D) Specifying the version of the program.

10. True or False: In Java, it's unnecessary to understand the structure of the code, such as where classes and methods are defined.
    - True
    - False

Answers: 1.B 2.False 3.B 4.B 5.D 6.False 7.C 8. A 9. B 10. False

3.2 Java Packages

3.2.1 Understanding Java Packages

In Java, a package functions much like a folder, providing a way to organize related classes and interfaces within your codebase. By grouping similar classes together, packages enhance the organization and accessibility of your code, making it easier to manage and utilize. Java comes with built-in packages containing useful classes that can be readily incorporated into your programs. Additionally, you have the flexibility to create your own custom packages to further organize and structure your code according to your specific project requirements.

3.2.2 Using Built-in Packages

The `import` statement in Java allows you to include a package in your program, granting access to the classes and interfaces within that package. For instance, if you wish to utilize a class named `Scanner` from the `java.util` package, you can import it using the following syntax:

```
import java.util.Scanner;
```

This declaration indicates your intention to utilize the `Scanner` class from the `java.util` package within your program.

3.2.3 Importing Classes from Package

When working with Java packages, you often need to use specific classes or even all the classes within a package. You can do this by using the import keyword in your code.

- Importing a Specific Class: If you only need one class from a package, you can import it directly. For instance, to use the Scanner class from the java.util package, you would write:

```
import java.util.Scanner;
```

This statement allows you to use the Scanner class in your program.

enables access within the same package or by subclasses, and the default (no modifier) limits access to classes within the same package. Access modifiers play a crucial role in encapsulation, security, and maintaining code integrity in Java programs.

3.3.2.1 Public Modifier

`Public`: Anything marked `public` can be used by any other class.

The public modifier makes a member accessible from any other class, regardless of where it's being accessed from. If you declare a class or a method as public, it can be accessed from any other class.

3.3.2.2 Private Modifier

`Private`: If something is `private`, only the class it's in can use it.

The private modifier restricts the visibility to only within the class where it's declared. It's the most restrictive access level. Private members cannot be accessed directly from outside their own class.

3.3.2.3 Protected Modifier

`Protected`: `Protected` items can be used in the same package and by subclasses.

The protected modifier allows the access within the same package and also by subclasses. Protected members are more accessible than private but more restrictive than public.

3.3.2.4 Default Modifier

`Default`: If you don't specify an access modifier, it's 'default', which means only classes in the same package can use it.

When no access modifier is specified, the default access level is applied. It allows the code to be accessed within the same package but not from outside this package.

3.3.3 Practical Example of Using Access Modifiers

Consider a class MyClass with different access modifiers applied to its methods:

```
class MyClass {
    public void publicMethod() {
        // Can be accessed from any class
    }

    private void privateMethod() {
        // Only accessible within MyClass
    }

    protected void protectedMethod() {
        // Accessible within the same package and subclasses
    }

    void defaultMethod() {
        // Accessible only within the same package
    }
}
```

In this example, `publicMethod` can be accessed from any class, `privateMethod` is only accessible within `MyClass`, `protectedMethod` can be accessed from subclasses and within the same package, and `defaultMethod` is accessible only within its package.

3.4. Practical Examples and Usage

3.4.1. Applying Naming Conventions in Code

Understanding and applying naming conventions is crucial for writing clear and maintainable Java code. Let's consider an example:

```
class ElectricCar {
    private int batteryLife;

    public ElectricCar(int initialBatteryLife) {
        batteryLife = initialBatteryLife;
    }

    public void chargeBattery() {
        batteryLife = 100;
    }
}
```

In this example, `ElectricCar` (class name) uses TitleCase, `batteryLife` (variable) uses camelCase, and `chargeBattery` (method) also uses camelCase, following Java naming conventions.

3.4.2. Using Packages in Code

Packages in Java help organize your classes and avoid name conflicts. Here's an example of how to use packages:

```
package vehicles;

class Car {
    // Car class code goes here
}

public class TestCar {
    public static void main(String[] args) {
        vehicles.Car myCar = new vehicles.Car();
        // Test the Car class functionality
    }
}
```

In this example, the `Car` class is part of the `vehicles` package, demonstrating how packages can be used to organize classes.

3.4.3. Applying Access Modifiers

Access modifiers determine the visibility of classes, methods, and variables in Java.

3.4.3.1. Public Access Example

```
public class PublicExample {
    public void display() {
        System.out.println("Public Access");
    }
}
```

Here, the display method is public, so it can be accessed from any other class.

3.4.3.2. Private Access Example

```
public class PrivateExample {
    private int data = 10;

    private void display() {
        System.out.println("Private Access: " + data);
    }
}
```

In PrivateExample, both the data variable and the display method are private, meaning they cannot be accessed outside this class.

3.4.3.3. Protected Access Example

```
class Base {
    protected void display() {
        System.out.println("Protected Access");
    }
}

public class ProtectedExample extends Base {
    public static void main(String[] args) {
        ProtectedExample obj = new ProtectedExample();
        obj.display();  // Accessing protected method
    }
}
```

In this example, the display method is protected in the base class and accessed by the subclass ProtectedExample.

Summary of Key Concepts

In Java, effectively managing and safeguarding your code is fundamental to developing robust applications. Chapter 3 introduces two critical concepts in Java programming that serve this purpose: packages and access modifiers. These concepts are essential for organizing your code into a coherent structure and controlling its visibility and accessibility across different parts of your application.

Packages: Packages in Java are used to group related classes, interfaces, and sub-packages, thereby providing a structured hierarchy that helps manage large codebases. By using packages, developers can easily organize code modules, avoid naming conflicts among classes, and control access levels.

This hierarchical organization makes it easier for developers to locate and use the classes they need, enhances code reusability, and facilitates maintenance. For instance, Java's standard library is divided into packages such as `java.util` for utility classes and `java.io` for input/output operations, showcasing how packages can categorize functionality.

Access Modifiers: Access modifiers in Java define the scope of accessibility for classes, methods, constructors, and variables. They are the primary means of implementing encapsulation, one of the four pillars of Object-Oriented Programming (OOP). The four access levels provided by Java-private, default (no modifier), protected, and public-determine whether other classes can access a particular member field or method. For example, the `private` modifier restricts access to the declaring class only, fostering a design that hides the internal implementation details and protects the integrity of the data. On the other hand, the `public` modifier allows other classes to access the member, enabling interaction between different parts of a program.

Summary: Understanding and applying packages and access modifiers are foundational skills in Java programming. Packages help in organizing code into manageable segments, making development, maintenance, and navigation through the codebase more efficient. Access modifiers enforce encapsulation by controlling the visibility and accessibility of code elements, thereby safeguarding the internal data and implementation details from unintended access and modifications. Together, these concepts equip developers with the tools to structure their Java applications more effectively, promoting clean, modular, and secure coding practices. As beginners grasp these basics, they lay a strong foundation for building well-organized and robust Java applications.

Chapter 4: Dancing with Data – Variables and Data Types

In Java programming, a cornerstone concept is the use of variables. Variables act as containers or storage for data in your programs. Understanding variables and the various types of data they can hold is a critical step in mastering Java. This chapter will delve into the intricacies of variables and data types, providing a foundation for understanding how data is manipulated and stored in Java.

4.1 Understanding Variables and Data Types

4.1.1 What are Variables and Data Types?

A variable in Java is akin to a storage box where you can keep different types of items. The type of these items, whether they are numbers, characters, or even a series of characters (like words or sentences), is determined by the data type of the variable. For instance, a variable can hold an integer (whole number), or a character (like 'A'), or a boolean value (true or false).

Consider a program that counts the number of characters input by a user. We use a variable called '`count`' to store this number. The '`count`' variable is declared as an integer, as it will hold a whole number.

Here's a basic example of how a variable is used.

Example:

```
class Count {
    public static void main (String[] args) throws java.
io.IOException {
        int count = 0;
        while (System.in.read() != -1) {
            count++;
        }
        System.out.println("Input has " + count + " chars.");
    }
}
```

Explanation: In this code, `count` is an integer variable that keeps track of the number of characters entered.

4.1.2 Variable Types – Data Types

Every variable in Java has a data type. The data type of a variable dictates what kind of values it can hold and the operations that can be performed on it. For example, an 'int' (integer) type variable can hold whole numbers, both positive and negative, and you can perform arithmetic operations such as addition and subtraction on it.

Java classifies data types into two categories: primitive and non-primitive (or reference types). Primitive data types include:

- Integer types: `byte`, `short`, `int`, `long`
- Floating-point types: `float`, `double`
- Boolean type: `boolean`
- Character type: `char`

These are the basic building blocks of data manipulation in Java.

4.1.3 Check Your Understanding

1. **What does a variable in Java represent?**
   a) A method in a program
   b) A data storage area
   c) A type of data type
   d) A specific value of an integer

2. **Which of the following is NOT a primitive data type in Java?**
   a) String
   b) int
   c) boolean
   d) double

3. **In the given code int count = 0;, what is count?**
   a) A method
   b) A class
   c) A variable
   d) A data type

4. **What kind of data does the boolean data type store?**
   a) Whole numbers
   b) True or false values
   c) Decimal numbers
   d) Characters

5. **Which data type would you use to store a single character?**
   a) int
   b) boolean
   c) char
   d) String

Answer Key: 1. b - A data storage area; 2. a - `String`; 3. c - A variable
4. b - True or false values; 5. c - `char`

4.2 How They Work in Java – Variable Names

In Java, variables are identified by their names. When we want to perform an operation on a variable, we refer to it by the name we've given it. The naming convention in Java is quite straightforward but essential. Variable names usually start with a lowercase letter, and if the name contains multiple words, each subsequent word starts with an uppercase letter, a style known as camelCase.

The way we name variables in Java is not just for convenience; it follows a convention. Variable names typically start with a lowercase letter, and if the name comprises multiple words, we use camelCase. For instance, `myNumber`, `totalAmount`, and `isAvailable` are examples of standard Java variable naming.

4.2.1 Check Your Understanding

1. **Which of the following is true about variable names in Java?**
   a) They must start with a number.
   b) They are not case-sensitive.
   c) They can contain spaces.
   d) They follow camelCase convention for multiple words.

2. **What is the initial letter case for a Java variable name?**
   a) Capital
   b) Lowercase
   c) It doesn't matter
   d) Special characters

3. **Which of these is a valid Java variable name?**
   a) `3days`
   b) `myHeight`
   c) `boolean`
   d) `java-class`

4. **In Java, which naming convention is used for variables?**
   a) PascalCase
   b) camelCase
   c) snake_case
   d) kebab-case
5. **What does the camelCase naming convention mean?**
   a) Starting every word with a capital letter
   b) Using an underscore between words
   c) Starting the first word with a lowercase letter, and capitalizing the first letter of each
   subsequent word
   d) Capitalizing all letters

Answers: 1. d - They follow camelCase convention for multiple words.
2. b - Lowercase 3. b - myHeight 4. b - camelCase
5. c - Starting the first word with a lowercase letter, and capitalizing the first letter of each subsequent word

4.3 Scope of Variables

The scope of a variable is essentially the part of the program where the variable is accessible. Java defines several scopes for variables:

- Local Variables: These are declared within a method and are accessible only within the confines of that method.
- Instance Variables: Declared within a class but outside any method, these variables are accessible by all methods in the class.
- Static Variables: Declared with the static keyword, these variables are shared among all instances of the class.

Understanding the scope of variables is crucial for properly managing how and where data is accessible within your program.
The scope of a variable is determined by where it is declared. In Java, there are mainly three kinds of variable scopes: local, instance, and class level (static variables). Local variables are declared within methods and are only accessible within those methods. Instance variables are declared in a class but outside any method and are accessible by all methods in the class. Static variables are declared with the static keyword and are shared among all instances of the class.

Understanding these different types of variables is crucial for managing how data is stored and modified within your Java programs. It allows you to control the access level of your data and ensures that your program behaves as expected.

As you continue your journey in Java programming, keep in mind the power and flexibility that variables offer. They are the building blocks of any Java program and mastering their use is key to becoming proficient in Java programming. The next step in your journey will be exploring how to control the flow of your programs, making them more dynamic and interactive.

4.3.1 Check Your Understanding

1. **Where is a local variable accessible?**
   a) Anywhere in the class it is declared
   b) Only within the method where it is declared
   c) In any method of the program
   d) Throughout all classes of the package

2. **Which type of variable is accessible throughout all methods in the class where it is declared?**
   a) Local variable
   b) Instance variable
   c) Static variable
   d) External variable

3. **What is the scope of a static variable?**
   a) Only in the method where it is declared
   b) Throughout the entire program
   c) Only in the class where it is declared
   d) In the package of the class

4. **If a variable is declared within a loop inside a method, when is it destroyed?**
   a) After the program ends
   b) As soon as it is used once
   c) When the method finishes execution
   d) At the end of the loop execution

5. **Where can an instance variable be accessed from within its class?**
   a) Only in the constructor
   b) Only in static methods

c) In all methods and constructors
d) Only in private methods

Answer Key: 1. b - Only within the method where it is declared;
2. b - Instance variable 3. c - Only in the class where it is declared;
4. d - At the end of the loop execution 5. c - In all methods and constructors

4.4 Types of Variables

Java has different types of variables, each with its own use case:

4.4.1 Local Variables

Local variables are defined within methods and are only accessible within those methods. They are created when the method is called and destroyed when the method exits.

Example & Exercise:

```
public class Example {
    public static void main(String[] args) {
        int localVar = 10; // 'localVar' is a local variable
        System.out.println("Local Variable: " + localVar);
    }
}
```

Output: `Local Variable Value: 10`

Fun Exercise: Character Mood Changes

Try modifying the value of `localVar` within the `main` method and observe the changes in the output. Compile and run this as a project in Apache NetBeans to see if you get the expected results.

Example Program

```
public class BasicVariablesExample {
    public static void main(String[] args) {
        // Declare and initialize an integer variable
        int age = 25;

        // Declare a double variable and initialize it
        double height = 5.9;

        // Declare a boolean variable and initialize it
        boolean isAdult = age >= 18;

        // Declare and initialize a String variable
        String name = "Alice";

        // Print the variables
        System.out.println("Name: " + name);
        System.out.println("Age: " + age);
        System.out.println("Height: " + height + " feet");
        System.out.println("Is Adult: " + isAdult);

        // Modify the age variable and print the updated value
        age = 30;
        System.out.println("Updated Age: " + age);
    }
}
```

Output:

```
Name: Alice
Age: 25
Height: 5.9 feet
Is Adult: true
Updated Age: 30
```

Explanation:

- Variable Declaration and Initialization: This program introduces four basic types of variables (`int, double, boolean, and String`), demonstrating how to declare and immediately initialize them with values.
- Printing Variables: It shows how to use variables in operations, here to concatenate strings and variables to print meaningful statements.

This demonstrates how variables hold data that can be used throughout a program.

- Modifying Variables: By updating the age variable partway through the program, it illustrates that variables' values can change, and those changes are reflected in any subsequent use of the variable.
- Basic Data Types and Operations: This example covers a spectrum of basic data types and includes a simple operation (`age >= 18`) to derive a boolean value, showcasing how variables can interact and be used in expressions.
- Engagement and Experimentation: Readers can be encouraged to modify the values of the variables, add more variables, or incorporate more operations to see direct impacts on the program's output, fostering interaction and deeper understanding.

4.4.2 Instance Variables

Instance variables belong to an instance of a class. Each object has its own copy of these variables.

Example & Exercise:

```
public class InstanceVarExample {
    int instanceVar; // 'instanceVar' is an instance variable

    public static void main(String[] args) {
        InstanceVarExample obj = new InstanceVarExample();
        obj.instanceVar = 5;
        System.out.println("Instance Variable Value: " + obj.
instanceVar);
    }
}
```

Expected Output: `Instance Variable Value: 5`

Fun Exercise:

Create multiple objects of `InstanceVarExample class`, assign different values to `instanceVar` for each object, and print them. Run this in Apache NetBeans and check if each object retains its unique value.

Example Program

```
public class InstanceVarExample {
    // Instance variable unique to each object
    int instanceVar;

    // Constructor to set the magic number for each character
    public InstanceVarExample(int magicNumber) {
        this.instanceVar = magicNumber;
    }

    public void displayMagicNumber() {
        System.out.println("Magic number is: " + instanceVar);
    }

    public static void main(String[] args) {
        // Create characters with their unique magic numbers
        InstanceVarExample alice = new InstanceVarExample(7);
        InstanceVarExample bob = new InstanceVarExample(13);
        InstanceVarExample charlie = new
InstanceVarExample(22);

        // The story begins
        System.out.println("In a mystical land, three friends
discovered their magic numbers...");

        System.out.print("Alice's ");
        alice.displayMagicNumber();

        System.out.print("Bob's ");
        bob.displayMagicNumber();

        System.out.print("Charlie's ");
        charlie.displayMagicNumber();

        System.out.println("With their unique magic numbers,
they set out on an adventure to uncover the secrets of the
mystical land!");
    }
}
```

Expected Output:
```
In a mystical land, three friends discovered their mag-
ic numbers...
Alice's Magic number is: 7
Bob's Magic number is: 13
Charlie's Magic number is: 22
With their unique magic numbers, they set out on an ad-
venture to uncover the secrets of the mystical land!
```

Explanation:

- **Character Creation**: Each character (Alice, Bob, Charlie) is created as an instance of `InstanceVarExample`, with a unique magic number assigned to them through the constructor.
- **Revealing Magic Numbers**: The story introduces the characters and their magic numbers, making it engaging by tying the concept of instance variables to a story element.
- **Adventure Begins**: The final print statement hints at a beginning adventure, tying back to how their unique magic numbers (instance variables) might play a role.

This approach makes the concept of instance variables fun and memorable by embedding it within a narrative context.

Fun Exercise For Over Achievers
Write a program for the following scenario.
For this fun exercise, let's create a scenario where we have a character whose mood changes based on the value of a local variable. We'll modify the mood value within the main method and observe how this change affects our character's mood description.

Example Java Program: Character Mood Changes

```
public class MoodExample {
    // Method to describe mood based on the value
    public static void describeMood(int moodValue) {
        String mood;
        if(moodValue < 5) {
            mood = "Sad";
        } else if(moodValue <= 10) {
            mood = "Happy";
        } else {
            mood = "Ecstatic";
        }
        System.out.println("With a mood value of " + moodValue
+ ", the character is feeling " + mood + ".");
    }

    public static void main(String[] args) {
        // Initial mood value
        int moodValue = 3;
        System.out.println("In the morning:");
        describeMood(moodValue);

        // Change the mood value
        moodValue = 7;
        System.out.println("In the afternoon:");
        describeMood(moodValue);

        // Change the mood value again
        moodValue = 12;
        System.out.println("In the evening:");
        describeMood(moodValue);
    }
}
```

Expected Output:

```
In the morning:
With a mood value of 3, the character is feeling Sad.
In the afternoon:
With a mood value of 7, the character is feeling Happy.
In the evening:
With a mood value of 12, the character is feeling Ecstatic.
```

Explanation:

- Mood Description: The `describeMood` method takes a local variable `moodValue` as input and decides the character's mood based on this value. The mood descriptions change according to the value of `moodValue`.
- Local Variable Modification: Within the `main` method, we modify the value of the local variable `moodValue` to simulate changes in our character's mood throughout the day.
- Fun Storytelling: This approach creates a fun narrative around how a character's mood changes throughout the day, making the concept of local variable modification engaging and memorable.

4.4.3 Static Variables

Static variables are shared among all instances of the class and are declared using the `static` keyword. They are created when the program starts and destroyed when the program stops.

Example & Exercise:

```
public class StaticVarExample {
    static int staticVar; // 'staticVar' is a static variable

    public static void main(String[] args) {
        StaticVarExample.staticVar = 10;
        System.out.println("Static Variable Value: " +
StaticVarExample.staticVar);

        StaticVarExample anotherInstance = new
StaticVarExample();
        anotherInstance.staticVar = 20;
        System.out.println("Static Variable Updated Value: " +
StaticVarExample.staticVar);
    }
}
```

Output:
```
Static Variable Value: 10
Static Variable Updated Value: 20
```

Fun Exercise:

Modify `staticVar` using different instances of `StaticVarExample` and observe how the change is reflected across all instances. Execute this code in Apache NetBeans and note how the static variable retains the last updated value, regardless of which object modified it.

Example Program

```
public class StaticVarExample {
    // Static variable shared by all instances
    static int staticVar = 0;

    public void displayVar() {
        System.out.println("The current value of staticVar is:
" + staticVar);
    }

    public void incrementStaticVar() {
        staticVar++;
    }

    public static void main(String[] args) {
        // Create the first instance of StaticVarExample
        StaticVarExample instance1 = new StaticVarExample();
        instance1.displayVar(); // Display the initial value

        // Increment staticVar using instance1
        instance1.incrementStaticVar();
        instance1.displayVar(); // Display the changed value

        // Create the second instance of StaticVarExample
        StaticVarExample instance2 = new StaticVarExample();
        instance2.displayVar(); // This will show the updated
staticVar value

        // Increment staticVar using instance2
        instance2.incrementStaticVar();
        instance1.displayVar(); // Display the updated value
using instance1
        instance2.displayVar(); // Display the updated value
using instance2
    }
}
```

Output:
```
The current value of staticVar is: 0
The current value of staticVar is: 1
The current value of staticVar is: 1
The current value of staticVar is: 2
The current value of staticVar is: 2
```

These exercises will help solidify your understanding of local, instance, and static variables in Java. Remember to create a project in Apache NetBeans for each exercise to verify your results and enhance your learning experience.

Understanding these variable types is crucial for data storage and manipulation in Java. In the next section, we'll explore how to create variables and assign values to them, further demystifying how Java handles data.

4.4.4 Check Your Understanding

1. **Local Variable Scope: Where can a local variable be accessed in Java?**
   a) Anywhere in its class
   b) Only within the method where it is declared
   c) Across different classes in the same package
   d) Throughout the entire program

2. **Instance Variable Characteristics: Which statement is true about instance variables in Java?**
   a) They are shared among all instances of a class.
   b) They are declared inside methods.
   c) Each instance of a class has its own copy of instance variables.
   d) They are destroyed as soon as a method call is completed.

3. **Static Variables: When are static variables created and destroyed in a Java program?**
   a) With the creation and destruction of each object of the class
   b) With the start and end of the program execution
   c) At the beginning and end of each method call
   d) When they are first used and when the class is unloaded

4. **Variable Accessibility: Which type of variable is accessible to all methods in a class without creating an instance of the class?**
   a) Local variable
   b) Instance variable
   c) Static variable
   d) Public variable

5. **Static vs. Instance Variables: What is a major difference between static and instance variables?**
   a) Static variables can change values across different instances, while instance variables cannot.
   b) Instance variables are shared among all instances of a class, while static variables are not.
   c) Static variables are associated with a class, while instance variables are associated with an object.
   d) Instance variables require explicit initialization, while static variables do not.

Answers: 1. c - They are shared among all instances of a class
2. c - The instance of the class is destroyed. 3. a - Local variable;
4. b - Instance variable; 5. c - Static variable

4.5 Creating Variables in Java

Creating a variable in Java is a simple process that involves declaring its type and assigning it a value. This step is fundamental in any Java program as it sets the foundation for data manipulation. Creating a variable in Java involves declaring its type and assigning it a value. The type can be any of the data types Java supports, such as `int` for integers, `String` for text, or `boolean` for true/false values. The name you give to your variable can be almost anything, but it's best to choose something that clearly describes what the variable represents.

Example of Variable Creation:

```
public class VariableCreation {
    public static void main(String[] args) {
        int number = 15;
        String text = "Learning Java";
        boolean flag = true;

        System.out.println("Number: " + number);
        System.out.println("Text: " + text);
        System.out.println("Flag: " + flag);
    }
}
```

Expected Output:

```
Number: 15
Text: Learning Java
Flag: true
```

Fun Exercise:

Using the above `VariableCreation` program, try changing the values of `number`, `text`, and `flag`. For instance, assign a different number to `number`, another sentence to `text`, and `false` to `flag`. Check the output after running your program in Apache NetBeans to see if it matches your changes.

4.5.1 Check Your Understanding

1. **Variable Declaration: What is the correct way to declare a variable in Java?**
   a) `type value = variableName;`
   b) `variableName = value;`
   c) `type variableName = value;`
   d) `variableName type = value;`

2. **Data Type Assignment: Which of these is a valid way to assign a value to an int variable in Java?**
   a) `int myNum = "123";`
   b) `int myNum = 123;`
   c) `int myNum = 123.0;`
   d) `int myNum = true;`

3. **String Variable Initialization: How do you correctly initialize a String variable in Java?**
   a) `String myString = 'Hello';`
   b) `String myString = Hello;`
   c) `String myString = "Hello";`
   d) `String = "Hello" myString;`

4. **Boolean Data Type: Which of the following is the correct way to declare a boolean variable in Java?**
   a) `boolean isJavaFun = "true";`
   b) `boolean isJavaFun = 1;`
   c) `boolean isJavaFun = true;`
   d) `boolean isJavaFun = 'true';`

5. **Changing Variable Values: What happens if you change the value of a variable in Java?**
    a) The original value is kept.
    b) The new value replaces the original value.
    c) An error occurs.
    d) The variable is deleted.

Answer Key: 1. c - `type variableName = value;`
2. b - `int myNum = 123;` 3. c - `String myString = "Hello";`
4. c - `boolean isJavaFun = true;` 5. b - The new value replaces the original value.

4.6 Rules for Naming Variables

When naming variables in Java, following certain rules and conventions is crucial for code readability and to avoid errors. When naming variables in Java, there are a few rules and conventions to follow:

- Start with a Letter or Underscore: Variable names should begin with a letter (either uppercase or lowercase) or an underscore (_).
- Case Sensitivity: Java is case-sensitive, which means that `myVariable`, `MyVariable`, and `MYVARIABLE` are different variables.
- Use Descriptive Names: Choose names that describe the purpose of the variable, like `totalAmount`, `userName`, or `isFinished`.
- CamelCase for Multiple Words: If a variable name consists of multiple words, start it with a lowercase letter followed by uppercase letters for each new word, for example, `totalDistance` or `firstDayOfSchool`.

Integer Variable (int): numberOfApples
Double Variable (double): applePrice
Boolean Variable (boolean): isAppleInStock
String Variable (String): appleType
Printing Variables: System.out.println

Example and Exercise:

```
public class NamingVariables {
    public static void main(String[] args) {
        int playerScore = 100;
        String playerName = "Alex";
        boolean gameStarted = true;

        System.out.println("Player Name: " + playerName);
        System.out.println("Player Score: " + playerScore);
        System.out.println("Game Started: " + gameStarted);
    }
}
```

Output:

```
Player Name: Alex
Player Score: 100
Game Started: true
```

Fun Exercise:

Create your own variables using different data types and ensure they follow the Java naming conventions. For instance, create a double variable for a price, a char variable for an initial, and a boolean variable for a condition. Then, print out their values. You can verify your code's output by running the program in Apache NetBeans.

Example Program `VariableNamingConvention`

```
public class VariableNamingConvention {
    public static void main(String[] args) {
        // Integer variable for age
        int userAge = 30;

        // Double variable for height in meters
        double userHeightMeters = 1.75;

        // Boolean variable to check if user is adult
        boolean isUserAdult = true;

        // String variable for user's name
        String userName = "John Doe";
```

```
  // Display the variables
        System.out.println("User Name: " + userName);
        System.out.println("User Age: " + userAge);
        System.out.println("User Height (meters): " +
userHeightMeters);
        System.out.println("Is User Adult: " + isUserAdult);
    }
}
```

Expected Output:	Apple Type: Fuji Number of Apples: 5 Price per Apple: $0.99 Is Apple in Stock: true

Explanation:

- Class Declaration: The program defines a public class named `VariableNamingConvention`. In Java, the class name should start with an uppercase letter and follow the CamelCase convention, where each new word starts with an uppercase letter.
- Main Method: It contains the main method, which is the entry point of any Java program. The syntax `public static void main(String[] args)` is standard for any Java application.
- Variable Declarations:
- Integer Variable (`int`): `numberOfApples` holds the number of apples, demonstrating an integer data type usage. The variable name is descriptive and follows camelCase, starting with a lowercase letter and each subsequent word starting with an uppercase letter.
- Double Variable (`double`): `applePrice` represents the price of an apple. It uses the `double` data type for decimal values, adhering to the same naming convention for readability.
- Boolean Variable (`boolean`): `isAppleInStock` indicates whether apples are in stock. The name is prefixed with `is`, which is a common convention for boolean variables to signify a yes/no or true/false value.
- String Variable (`String`): `appleType` contains the type of apple as a string of text. `String` variables hold text and, like other variables, follow camelCase naming.
- Printing Variables: The `System.out.println` statements are used to output the values of the variables to the console. It demonstrates how to concatenate strings with variables to form a descriptive message.

These exercises are designed to give you hands-on experience with creating and naming variables in Java. Remember, practicing in an IDE like Apache NetBeans will not only help you see the immediate output of your code but also familiarize you with a professional development environment.

4.6.1 Check Your Understanding

1. **What is the correct way to name a variable that stores the number of students?**
   a) `int 1students;`
   b) `int number_of_students;`
   c) `int numberOfStudents;`
   d) `int Number Of Students;`

2. **Which of the following variables is different in Java's case-sensitive environment?**
   a) `userLogin`
   b) `Userlogin`
   c) `userlogin`
   d) `userLogin` and `userlogin` are the same

3. **Which of these is a recommended practice for naming variables in Java?**
   a) Using abbreviations
   b) Starting with a number
   c) Using complete words to describe the variable's purpose
   d) Starting with special characters like $ or _

4. **For a variable that stores a city name, which naming is appropriate?**
   a) `String 1city;`
   b) `String City;`
   c) `String city_name;`
   d) `String cityName;`

5. **Can you use class as a variable name in Java?**
   a) Yes
   b) No

Answers to Section 4.6: 1. c - `int numberOfStudents;`
2. b - `Userlogin` 3. c - Using complete words to describe the variable's purpose; 4. d - `String cityName;` 5. b - No

4.7 Working with Data Types

Data types are critical in Java as they define the kind of data a variable can hold and the operations that can be performed on them. Each primitive data type in Java serves a specific purpose:

- Integer Types (`byte`, `short`, `int`, `long`): Use these for numerical values without decimal points. `int` is the most commonly used for whole numbers.
- Floating-Point Types (`float`, `double`): These are for numbers with decimal points. `double` is more precise and commonly used for calculations.
- Boolean (`boolean`): This type is used for true/false values. It's often used in conditional statements.
- Character (`char`): It stores a single character and is useful in text processing.

Example of Using Different Data Types:

```
public class DataTypesExample {
    public static void main(String[] args) {
        int year = 2021;
        double temperature = 36.5;
        boolean isRaining = false;
        char grade = 'A';

        System.out.println("Year: " + year);
        System.out.println("Temperature: " + temperature);
        System.out.println("Is it raining? " + isRaining);
        System.out.println("Grade: " + grade);
    }
}
```

Output:

```
Year: 2021
Temperature: 36.5
Is it raining? false
Grade: A
```

Here, year is an integer, temperature is a floating-point number, `is Raining` is a boolean, and grade is a character.

Understanding and utilizing these data types effectively is key to writing robust and efficient Java programs. As you progress, you'll learn to manipulate these types in various ways to achieve the desired outcomes in your coding endeavors.

Fun Exercise:
Create a project in Apache NetBeans and replicate the above program. Try changing the values of each variable and observe the changes in the output. For instance, modify `year` to the current year, adjust `temperature` to your current environment's temperature, switch `isRaining` to `true` if it is raining, and change `grade` to a different letter. Execute the program to see if the output matches your expectations.

Example Program

```
public class DataTypesExample {
    public static void main(String[] args) {
        int year = 2024; // Updated year
        double temperature = 28.3; // Updated temperature
        boolean isRaining = false; // Updated weather condition
        char grade = 'B'; // Updated grade

        System.out.println("Year: " + year);
        System.out.println("Temperature: " + temperature);
        System.out.println("Is it raining? " + isRaining);
        System.out.println("Grade: " + grade);
    }
}
```

Expected Output:

```
Year: 2024
Temperature: 28.3
Is it raining? false
Grade: B
```

This exercise allows you to see how different data types are used in Java and how changing their values affects the program's output. Practicing in an environment like Apache NetBeans enhances your understanding and gives you a real-world experience of Java programming.

4.7.1 Check Your Understanding

1. **What is the correct way to declare an integer variable age with a value of 25?**

   a) `int age = "25";`

   b) `int age = 25;`

c) `float age = 25;`
d) `boolean age = 25;`

2. **Which of these is a floating-point variable correctly declared?**
   a) `float temp = 98.6;`
   b) `double temp = 98.6;`
   c) `int temp = 98.6;`
   d) `char temp = 98.6;`

3. **For a boolean variable isJavaFun that holds a true value, how should it be declared?**
   a) `boolean isJavaFun = "true";`
   b) `boolean isJavaFun = true;`
   c) `String isJavaFun = true;`
   d) `boolean isJavaFun = 'true';`

4. **How do you correctly declare a character variable grade with the value 'A'?**
   a) `char grade = "A";`
   b) `char grade = A;`
   c) `char grade = 'A';`
   d) `String grade = 'A';`

5. **How do you convert the integer 100 to a string in Java?**
   a) `String.valueOf(100);`
   b) `int.toString(100);`
   c) `String(100);`
   d) `"100";`

Answers: 1. b - `int age = 25;` 2.b - `double temp = 98.6;` 3. b - `boolean isJavaFun = true;` 4. c - `char grade = 'A';` 5. a - `String.valueOf(100);`

Summary of Key Concepts

Chapter 4 provided a comprehensive introduction to variables and data types in Java. We explored the concept of variables as containers for data and the importance of data types in defining the nature of data a variable can hold. The chapter emphasized the significance of variable naming conventions and the impact of scope on the accessibility of variables.

We distinguished between local, instance, and static variables, understanding their unique characteristics and use cases. The process of creating variables was explained, highlighting the importance of declaring the correct data type and following Java's naming rules.

Lastly, we delved into the various primitive data types available in Java, understanding their purpose and the kind of data they can store. This foundational knowledge of variables and data types is crucial for any Java programmer, as it forms the basis of data manipulation and storage in Java programming.

Key Concepts:

Understanding Variables and Data Types:

- Variables are fundamental in Java, serving as containers for storing data.
- Data types specify the kind of data a variable can hold, like integers, floating-point numbers, booleans, and characters.

Variable Names:

- Java uses camelCase naming convention for variables.
- Names should start with a lowercase letter and be descriptive.
- Case sensitivity is crucial in Java; `myVariable` and `MyVariable` are different.

Scope of Variables:

- Local Variables: Confined to the method they are declared in.
- Instance Variables: Belong to an instance of a class, accessible by all methods in the class.
- Static Variables: Class-level variables, shared across all instances.

Types of Variables:

- Local Variables: Declared within methods; their scope is limited to the method.
- Instance Variables: Declared in a class but outside methods; each instance has its copy.
- Static Variables: Declared with the static keyword; shared among all instances of the class.

Creating Variables in Java:

- Variables are declared by specifying a type followed by a name and optionally an initial value.
- The syntax follows the pattern: `type variableName = value;`

Rules for Naming Variables:

- Names should be meaningful and follow Java's naming conventions.
- Avoid using Java reserved keywords as variable names.

Working with Data Types:

- Primitive data types include integers (`int, byte, short, long`), floating-point (`float, double`), boolean (`boolean`), and character (`char`).
- Each data type serves a specific purpose and has a range of values it can store.

Chapter 5: Controlling the Flow of Your Programs

In this chapter, we'll explore how to control the flow of your Java programs using simple yet powerful concepts. These tools will help you decide what parts of your code should run and when.

5.1 Understanding Control Flow

5.1.1 What is Control Flow?

Control flow in programming involves providing your program with a map of what to do and when to do it. Imagine telling a friend a story where sometimes you say, "If this happens, then the story progresses accordingly, but if something else happens, the story changes."

5.1.2 Why Control Flow?

Without control flow, your programs would always do the same thing in the same order, which isn't very helpful. Control flow lets you make your program smarter and more useful by making decisions and repeating actions.

5.2 Types of Control Flow Statements

5.2.1 Decision-making Statements

These are like crossroads in your program where you can decide which way to go based on certain conditions. The two main types are:

- **If Statement**: It's like saying, "If this is true, then do this."
- **Switch Statement**: It's like choosing between several options.

Examples and Exercises

1. **Simple `if` Statement:**

```
int number = 10;
if (number > 5) {
    System.out.println("Number is greater than 5");
}
```

Exercise: Try changing the number to see different results.

2. **For Loop Example:**

```
for (int i = 0; i < 3; i++) {
    System.out.println("Loop iteration: " + i);
}
```

Exercise: Try changing 3 to another number and see how many times the loop runs.

3. Programming Exercise 1: Check for Positive Number

Task: Using NetBeans, write a Java program to check if a given number is positive. If the number is positive, print `"The number is positive."`

Example Code:

```
public class PositiveNumberCheck {
    public static void main(String[] args) {
        int number = 5; // You can change this value to test
with different numbers

        if (number > 0) {
            System.out.println("The number is positive.");
        }
    }
}
```

Expected Output (for `number = 5`): `The number is positive.`

Programming Exercise 2: Age Group Classification

Task: Using NetBeans, write a Java program to classify a person's age group. If the person is 18 years old or older, print "Adult". Otherwise, print "Minor".

Example Code:

```
public class AgeGroupClassification {
    public static void main(String[] args) {
        int age = 20; // You can change this value to test with
different ages

        if (age >= 18) {
            System.out.println("Adult");
        } else {
            System.out.println("Minor");
        }
    }
}
```

Expected Output (for `age = 20`): `Adult`

5.2.2 Loop Statements

Loops are like repeating a part of your story. They keep doing something over and over again until a certain condition is met. There are a few types:

- **For Loop**: Great for when you know how many times you want to repeat something.
- **While Loop**: Use this when you want to keep doing something as long as a condition is true.
- Do-While Loop: Similar to the while loop, but it always runs at least once.

Exercise 1: Counting Numbers with a `for` Loop
Task: Write a Java program to count from 1 to 5 using a for loop. Print each number on a new line.

Example Code:

```
public class CountingNumbers {
    public static void main(String[] args) {
        for (int i = 1; i <= 5; i++) {
            System.out.println(i);
        }
    }
}
```

Expected Output:	1 2 3 4 5

Exercise 2: Sum of Numbers Using a `while` Loop

Task: Write a Java program to calculate the sum of the first 5 natural numbers using a while loop.

Example Code:

```
public class SumOfNumbers {
    public static void main(String[] args) {
        int sum = 0;
        int i = 1;

        while (i <= 5) {
            sum += i;
            i++;
        }

        System.out.println("Sum is: " + sum);
    }
}
```

Expected Output: `Sum is: 15`

These exercises demonstrate the basic usage of `for` and `while` loops in Java. The `for` loop is used when the number of iterations is known beforehand, while the `while` loop is useful when the number of iterations is not known in advance but is determined by a condition. In the second exercise, the loop continues until i exceeds 5, summing up the numbers from 1 to 5.

5.2.3 Jump/Branching Statements

These let you skip parts of your code or stop a loop early. They're like shortcuts in your program.

Programming Exercise - "Guess the Number Game"

Task: Create a simple "Guess the Number" game where the program picks a random number between 1 and 100, and the user has to guess it. The program should provide hints like “Too high” or “Too low” after each guess. The game ends when the user guesses the number correctly.

Example Code:

```
import java.util.Scanner;
import java.util.Random;

public class GuessTheNumberGame {
    public static void main(String[] args) {
        Scanner scanner = new Scanner(System.in);
        Random random = new Random();
        int numberToGuess = random.nextInt(100) + 1;
        int numberOfTries = 0;
        int guess;
        boolean win = false;

        System.out.println("Guess a number between 1 and 100");

        while (!win) {
            guess = scanner.nextInt();
            numberOfTries++;

            if (guess == numberToGuess) {
                win = true;
            } else if (guess < numberToGuess) {
                System.out.println("Too low");
            } else if (guess > numberToGuess) {
                System.out.println("Too high");
            }
        }

        System.out.println("Congratulations! You guessed the
number in " + numberOfTries + " tries.");
    }
}
```

Expected Output: For the “Guess the Number Game,” the expected output will vary each time you run the program, as it depends on the random number generated and the guesses made by the user. However, here’s an example of how a typical game session might look:

```
Guess a number between 1 and 100
50
Too high
25
Too low
37
Too high
33
Too high
31
Congratulations! You guessed the number in 5 tries.
```

In this session:

- The random number to be guessed was 31.
- The player’s first guess was 50, which was too high.
- Subsequent guesses were 25 (too low), 37 and 33 (both too high).
- The player correctly guessed 31 on their fifth try.

Remember, in an actual game, the number to guess, the guesses, and the number of tries will differ each time.

Explanation:

- Import Statements: The program imports `Scanner` for reading user input and `Random` for generating a random number.
- Variables:
  - `numberToGuess`: The random number that the player has to guess.
  - `numberOfTries`: Keeps track of how many guesses the player has made.
  - `guess`: Stores the player’s current guess.
  - `win`: A boolean flag to check if the game has been won.
- Game Loop: The `while` loop continues until the player wins (`win` becomes `true`). Inside the loop:
  - The program takes the player’s guess as input.
  - Increments numberOfTries.

- Provides feedback based on the guess (too high, too low, or correct).

- Ending the Game: Once the correct number is guessed, the loop ends, and the program congratulates the player, showing the number of tries taken.

This exercise is fun and engaging for beginners, helping them understand control flow with loops and conditionals in a real-world application.

5.3 Fun Programming Exercises

Exercise 1: Traffic Light Simulator

Objective: In the NetBeans, create a simple program to simulate a traffic light. The traffic light changes from “Red” to “Green” to “Yellow”, and then back to “Red”. After displaying each color, the program should pause for a short duration.

Sample Code:

```
public class TrafficLightSimulator {
    public static void main(String[] args) throws
InterruptedException {
        String[] colors = {"Red", "Green", "Yellow"};
        while (true) {
            for (String color : colors) {
                System.out.println(color);
                Thread.sleep(2000); // Wait for 2 seconds
            }
        }
    }
}
```

Expected Output:

```
Red
Green
Yellow
Red
Green
Yellow
...
(continues indefinitely)
```

Explanation: The program uses an infinite loop to continuously cycle through the traffic light colors. The `Thread.sleep(2000)` makes the program wait for 2 seconds before changing to the next color, simulating a traffic light delay.

Exercise 2: Prime Number Finder

Objective: Write a program that asks the user for a number and then prints out all prime numbers up to that number.

Example Code:

```
import java.util.Scanner;

public class PrimeNumberFinder {
    public static void main(String[] args) {
        Scanner scanner = new Scanner(System.in);
        System.out.print("Enter a number: ");
        int number = scanner.nextInt();

        for (int i = 2; i <= number; i++) {
            if (isPrime(i)) {
                System.out.println(i + " is a prime number.");
            }
        }
    }

    private static boolean isPrime(int number) {
        for (int j = 2; j <= number / 2; j++) {
            if (number % j == 0) {
                return false;
            }
        }
        return true;
    }
}
```

Sample Run:

```
Enter a number: 10
2 is a prime number.
3 is a prime number.
5 is a prime number.
7 is a prime number.
```

Explanation: The program prompts the user for a number and then iterates through all numbers from 2 to the user's number. For each number, it checks if the number is prime using the `isPrime` function. If a number is prime, it prints a message stating that the number is a prime number. The `isPrime` function works by checking if the number is divisible by any number from 2 to half of its value. If it is, the function returns `false`, indicating that the number is not prime.

5.4 Check Your Understanding - Exercises and Answers

1. **What does the following loop do?**

```
for (int i = 0; i < 5; i++) {
    System.out.println(i);
}
```

   a) Prints numbers 0 to 4
   b) Prints numbers 1 to 5
   c) Causes an error

2. **What will the following code print?**

```
int x = 3;
if (x > 2) {
    System.out.println("Yes");
} else {
    System.out.println("No");
}
```

   a) Yes
   b) No
   c) Error

3. **Which statement in Java can be used to repeatedly execute a block of code as long as a particular condition is true?**
   a) `switch`
   b) `if-else`
   c) `while`
   d) `break`

4. **In a `for` loop, which part is executed only once at the beginning of the loop?**
   a) Increment statement

b) Condition check
c) Initialization
d) The code inside the loop

5. **What is the output of the following code snippet?**

```
int x = 3;
if (x > 2) {
    System.out.println("Yes");
} else {
    System.out.println("No");
}
```

a) `2`
b) `3`
c) The code will not compile.
d) The code will result in an infinite loop.

6. **Which of the following is true about the `break` statement in Java?**
a) It is used to exit a loop.
b) It sends the program back to the start of the loop.
c) It pauses the execution of the loop for a specified time.
d) It is used to skip the current iteration of a loop.

7. **What does the `continue` statement do in a loop?**
a) Stops the loop immediately.
b) Skips the current iteration and proceeds to the next iteration.
c) Continues to execute the current iteration indefinitely.
d) E*xits the program.*

Answer: 1. a. Prints numbers 0 to 4; 2. a. Yes; 3. c) `while;` 4. c) Initialization; 5. b) `3;` 6. a) It is used to exit a loop; 7. b) Skips the current iteration and proceeds to the next iteration.

Summary of Key Concepts

Chapter 5 covered the basics of controlling the flow of a Java program. You learned about making decisions with if and switch statements, repeating actions with loops like for and while, and changing the course of execution with jump statements like break. These concepts are fundamental in Java programming and will help you write more dynamic and interactive programs. Remember, practice is key, so try out these examples and exercises in your coding environment!

Mid-Book Review Request

Keeping the Java Brewing

"No matter which field of work you want to go in, it is of great importance to learn at least one programming language." — Ram Ray

Having read this far, you know how valuable learning Java programming is... and having found this book in the first place, I'm also sure you know how daunting it is when you come at it as a beginner.

There's so much information out there, and until you get to know the language, it can seem impossible to find an entry point. In fact, this is so much the case that many people abandon ship before they've even gotten started.

Having skills in Java programming opens so many doors. It improves your employability, and it opens up your understanding of a wide range of programming issues. My goal is to make it accessible to more people, and now that your confidence is growing, I'd like to ask you to help me.

Thankfully, this is easier than you might fear. All you have to do is leave your feedback online, and immediately, you'll make it easier for others to find the doorway to Java programming. Your thoughts at the mid-point are very much appreciated.

https://www.amazon.com/review/review-your-purchases/?asin=B0DFV594TD

By leaving a review of this book on Amazon, you'll show the people who are looking for accessible and straightforward information they can put to use immediately exactly where they can find it.

It's hard to imagine that something as small as a review could have such power, but it really does help information become more visible to the people who are already searching for it.

Thank you for your support. Now, let's get back into it, shall we?

Chapter 6: Methods, Objects, and Classes

One of the more confusing topics for Java beginners is understanding the difference between objects and classes and how they relate to each other. This chapter focuses on creating and calling methods, understanding classes and objects, and provides a mini-project to apply these concepts.

6.1 Introduction to Methods in Java

6.1.1 What are Methods?

Methods in Java are like actions. They are blocks of code that perform a specific task. Imagine you have a robot. You can program methods into it like `speak()` or `move()`, and whenever you tell it to `speak()` or `move()`, it will do those actions.

6.1.2 Why Use Methods?

Methods help you organize your code. Instead of writing the same code over and over again, you write it once in a method and then just call the method whenever you need it. This makes your code shorter, cleaner, and easier to understand.

6.1.3 Creating Methods in Java

To create a method, you need to decide what it will do, what it will be called, and what information it needs to do its job. In Java, you write methods inside classes.

6.1.4 Types of Methods

In Java, there are two types of methods: predefined methods and user-defined methods. Predefined methods are those that Java provides, such as `println()` for printing text. On the other hand, user-defined methods are ones that you create yourself to perform specific tasks.

6.1.5 Practical Exercise: Hello World Method

Create a method called `sayHello` that prints “`Hello, Universe!`”.

```
public class HelloUniverse {
    public static void sayHello() {
        System.out.println("Hello, Universe!");
    }

    public static void main(String[] args) {
        sayHello(); // Calling the method
    }
}
```

Expected Output: When you run this program, it should print "`Hello, Universe!`".

6.2 Understanding Objects and Classes

6.2.1 Basic Concepts

In Java, everything revolves around two key concepts: classes and objects.

- Classes are like blueprints. They describe how something should be made. For instance, a Bicycle class will describe what a bicycle is and what it can do.
- Objects are the actual things you create using those blueprints. So, if you create a new Bicycle from the Bicycle class, that new bicycle is an object.

6.2.2 Creating Your First Class

Here's how you make a simple class:

```
class Bicycle {
    int speed; // This is a field. It holds data about the
bicycle.

    void increaseSpeed() { // This is a method. It describes
what the bicycle can do.
        speed++;
    }
}
```

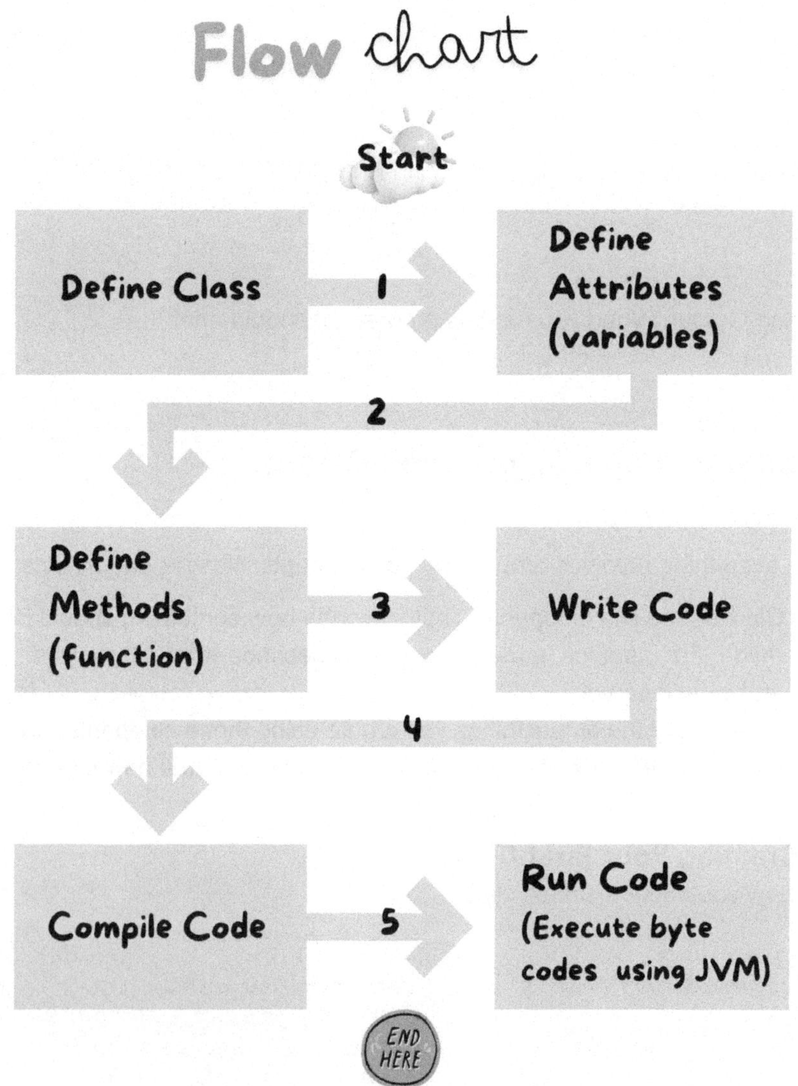

Explanation:

Class Declaration: `class Bicycle { ... }`

- This line declares a new class named `Bicycle`. A class in Java is like a blueprint or a template that describes the behavior (methods) and state (fields) of its objects.

Field Declaration: `int speed;`

- Here, we declare a field named `speed` with the data type `int` (integer). This field is a variable that belongs to the class `Bicycle` and it's used to store the speed of a bicycle. Fields represent the state or attributes of an object.
- In this case, `speed` is a simple integer value that will hold the current speed of the bicycle.

Method Declaration: `void increaseSpeed() { ... }`

- This is a method named `increaseSpeed`. Methods in a class define the behavior or actions that objects of the class can perform.
- The keyword `void` before the method name indicates that this method does not return any value.
- Inside the method, we have `speed++;`. This is an action or command telling the program to increase the `speed` field by 1. The `++` is an increment operator in Java, which increases the value of a variable by one.

How It Works:

- When you create an object of the `Bicycle` class, that object will have its own `speed` field, which it can manipulate using the `increaseSpeed` method.
- Initially, the `speed` of a new `Bicycle` object will be `0` (if not explicitly set to some other value) since `int` fields in Java default to `0`.
- Each time the `increaseSpeed` method is called on a `Bicycle` object, the object's `speed` will increase by 1.

In Practice: If you create a Bicycle object in your program and call increaseSpeed on it multiple times, you can observe the speed increasing with each call. This class models a very simplified concept of a bicycle where you can only increase its speed.

6.2.3 Creating and Using Objects

To use a class, you create an object from it like this:

```
public class TestBicycle {
    public static void main(String[] args) {
        Bicycle myBike = new Bicycle(); // Creating a Bicycle
object
        myBike.increaseSpeed(); // Using the increaseSpeed
method
        System.out.println(myBike.speed); // Printing the speed
    }
}
```

Expected Output: When you run this program, it will print the bicycle's speed, which is 1 after increasing it once.

Exercise: Create a Lamp Class
Create a class `Lamp` with a method `turnOn` that sets a `isOn` field to `true` and prints "`Lamp is on`".

```
class Lamp {
    // Field to store the state of the lamp (on or off)
    boolean isOn;

    // Method to turn the lamp on
    void turnOn() {
        isOn = true;
        System.out.println("Lamp is on.");
    }

    // Method to turn the lamp off
    void turnOff() {
        isOn = false;
        System.out.println("Lamp is off.");
    }
}
```

Sample Answer: To use it, create a `Lamp` object and call `turnOn`.

Explanation:

Class Declaration: `class Lamp { ... }`

- The `Lamp` class is declared using the `class` keyword, followed by the name of the class (`Lamp`). Everything inside the curly braces `{ ... }` defines what the Lamp class is and what it can do.

Field Declaration: `boolean isOn;`

- Inside the `Lamp` class, there's a field named `isOn`. This field is of type `boolean`, meaning it can hold either `true` or `false`. This field represents whether the lamp is on (`true`) or off (`false`).

Method to Turn the Lamp On: `void turnOn() { ... }`

- This method, when called, will set the `isOn` field to `true`, indicating that the lamp is turned on.
- The `void` keyword indicates that the method doesn't return any value.
- Inside the method, `isOn = true;` changes the state of the lamp to on, and `System.out.println("Lamp is on.");` prints a message to the console.

Method to Turn the Lamp Off: `void turnOff() { ... }`

- Similar to the `turnOn` method, `turnOff` changes the state of the lamp. It sets `isOn` to false, indicating the lamp is off.
- It also prints "`Lamp is off.`" to the console to provide feedback about the action.

How It Works:

- An instance (object) of the Lamp class will have the ability to be either on or off, represented by the `isOn` field.
- The `turnOn` and `turnOff` methods allow the object's state to be changed and provide a message to the user about this change.

Usage: In a Java program, you can create an instance of the `Lamp` class and use its methods to change and display its state. For example:

```
public class TestLamp {
    public static void main(String[] args) {
        Lamp myLamp = new Lamp(); // Create a Lamp object
        myLamp.turnOn();          // Turn the lamp on
        myLamp.turnOff();         // Turn the lamp off
    }
}
```

Expected Output:

```
Lamp is on.
Lamp is off.
```

In this example, `myLamp` is an object of the `Lamp` class, and we are calling its `turnOn` and `turnOff` methods to change its state and print the state to the console.

Explanation:

1. `Lamp myLamp = new Lamp();` creates a new instance of the `Lamp` class.
2. `myLamp.turnOn();` calls the `turnOn` method, setting `isOn` to `true` and printing "`Lamp is on.`"
3. `myLamp.turnOff();` calls the `turnOff` method immediately after, setting `isOn` to false and printing "`Lamp is off.`"

Test Your Knowledge: Exercises and Answers

1. Methods Exercise

Create a method that takes two integers and returns their sum.

```
public class Calculator {
    public static int addNumbers(int a, int b) {
        return a + b;
    }

    public static void main(String[] args) {
        int result = addNumbers(5, 10);
        System.out.println("The sum is: " + result);
    }
}
```

Expected Output: "`The sum is: 15`".

2. Objects Exercise

Create an object `Dog` with methods `bark` and `sleep`.

```
class Dog {
    void bark() {
        System.out.println("Woof!");
    }

    void sleep() {
        System.out.println("Zzz...");
    }
}
```

Methods `bark and sleep`

```
public class TestDog {
    public static void main(String[] args) {
        Dog myDog = new Dog();
        myDog.bark();
        myDog.sleep();
    }
}
```

Object `Dog`

```
class Dog {
    void bark() {
        System.out.println("Woof!");
    }

    void sleep() {
        System.out.println("Zzz...");
    }

    public static void main(String[] args) {
        Dog myDog = new Dog(); // Create an instance of Dog
        myDog.bark(); // Invoke the bark method
        myDog.sleep(); // Invoke the sleep method
    }
}
```

Methods `bark` and `sleep` and Object `Dog`
Expected Output:

```
Woof!
"Zzz...".
```

Congratulations! You have learned about methods, objects, and classes in Java. With these basics, you are well on your way to writing your own Java programs. Remember, practice is key, so keep experimenting with what you've learned.

6.3 Creating and Using Objects

Objects are instances of classes. Think of a class as a blueprint for a house, and an object as the house built from that blueprint. To create an object in Java, you use the `new` keyword followed by the class name.

Example:
Imagine we have a class named Book. To create a Book object, we would do the following:

```
public class Book {
    String title;
    String author;

    // Constructor
    public Book(String title, String author) {
        this.title = title;
        this.author = author;
    }

    void displayInfo() {
        System.out.println("Title: " + title + ", Author: " +
author);
    }
}

public class TestBook {
    public static void main(String[] args) {
        Book myBook = new Book("Java for Beginners", "John
Doe");
        myBook.displayInfo();
    }
}
```

Expected Output: `Title: Java for Beginners, Author: John Doe`

Exercise: Create a class named `Calculator` with methods to add, subtract, multiply, and divide two numbers. Then, create an object of `Calculator` and use it to perform basic arithmetic operations.

Sample Calculator.java

```
public class Calculator {

    // Method to add two numbers
    public int add(int num1, int num2) {
        return num1 + num2;
    }

    // Method to subtract two numbers
    public int subtract(int num1, int num2) {
        return num1 - num2;
    }

    // Method to multiply two numbers
    public int multiply(int num1, int num2) {
        return num1 * num2;
    }

    // Method to divide two numbers
    public double divide(double num1, double num2) {
        if(num2 != 0) {
            return num1 / num2;
        } else {
            System.out.println("Error: Division by zero");
            return 0;
        }
    }
}
```

Let's write a simple `Calculator` class that performs basic arithmetic operations such as addition, subtraction, multiplication, and division. Then, we'll create a `TestCalculator` class to test these operations.

Example Program TestCalculator.java

```
public class TestCalculator {
    public static void main(String[] args) {
        Calculator myCalc = new Calculator(); // Create a
Calculator object

        // Test addition
        System.out.println("5 + 3 = " + myCalc.add(5, 3));

        // Test subtraction
        System.out.println("5 - 3 = " + myCalc.subtract(5, 3));

        // Test multiplication
        System.out.println("5 * 3 = " + myCalc.multiply(5, 3));

        // Test division
        System.out.println("5 / 3 = " + myCalc.divide(5, 3));
    }
}
```

When you run the `TestCalculator` class, the Expected Output will be:

5 + 3 = 8
5 - 3 = 2
5 * 3 = 15
5 / 3 = 1.6666666666666667

6.4 Introduction to Inheritance

Inheritance allows a class to inherit properties and methods from another class. The class that inherits is called a subclass, and the class being inherited from is called a superclass.

Example:

```
class Vehicle {  // Superclass
    public void display() {
        System.out.println("This is a Vehicle");
    }
}
```

```
class Car extends Vehicle {  // Subclass
    public void display() {
        super.display();  // Calls the display method of
Vehicle
        System.out.println("This is a Car");
    }
}

public class TestInheritance {
    public static void main(String[] args) {
        Car myCar = new Car();
        myCar.display();
    }
}
```

Expected Output:

```
This is a Vehicle
This is a Car
```

For the given example, when you instantiate a `Car` object and call the `display()` method on it, the method in the `Car` class first calls the `display()` method of its superclass `Vehicle` using `super.display();`, and then executes its own print statement. Therefore, the expected output will be as shown above.

Exercise: Create a superclass named `Animal` and a subclass named `Dog`. The `Animal` class should have a method `makeSound` and the `Dog` class should override this method to print "`Bark`".

Expected Output for Exercise: When you create an object of Dog and call the makeSound method, it should display "`Bark`".

Example Program `Animal`

```
// Superclass Animal
class Animal {
    // Method in the superclass
    public void makeSound() {
        System.out.println("Some animal sound");
    }
}
```

```
// Subclass Dog extending Animal
class Dog extends Animal {
    // Overriding the makeSound method
    @Override
    public void makeSound() {
        System.out.println("Bark");
    }
}

// Test class to run the program
public class TestAnimalSound {
    public static void main(String[] args) {
        // Creating an object of the Dog class
        Dog myDog = new Dog();
        // Calling the makeSound method on the Dog object
        myDog.makeSound(); // This will execute the overridden
method in Dog class
    }
}
```

Expected Output: `Bark`

When you run the program and create an object of `Dog` and call the `makeSound` method, it will display "Bark", demonstrating polymorphism where the `Dog` class overrides the behavior of the `makeSound` method defined in the `Animal` superclass.

6.5 Introduction to Polymorphism

Polymorphism allows methods to do different things based on the object it is acting upon, even if the method shares the same name.

Example:

```
class Animal {
    public void sound() {
        System.out.println("Some sound");
    }
}
```

```
class Cat extends Animal {
    public void sound() {
        System.out.println("Meow");
    }
}

public class TestPolymorphism {
    public static void main(String[] args) {
        Animal myAnimal = new Cat();  // Polymorphism
        myAnimal.sound();
    }
}
```

Expected Output: `Meow`

Exercise: Extend the Animal class with another subclass named `Cow` that overrides the `sound` method to print "Moo". Create objects of both `Cow` and `Cat` and call their `sound` method.

Expected Output for Exercise: "Moo" for `Cow` and "Meow" for `Cat`.

```
class Animal {
    public void sound() {
        System.out.println("Some sound");
    }
}

class Cat extends Animal {
    @Override
    public void sound() {
        System.out.println("Meow");
    }
}

class Cow extends Animal {
    @Override
    public void sound() {
        System.out.println("Moo");
    }
}
```

```
public class TestPolymorphismExtended {
    public static void main(String[] args) {
        Animal myCat = new Cat(); // Create a Cat object
        myCat.sound();            // This should print "Meow"

        Animal myCow = new Cow(); // Create a Cow object
        myCow.sound();            // This should print "Moo"
    }
}
```

Expected Output:

```
Meow
Moo
```

When you run the `TestPolymorphismExtended` class, the output will be as shown above. This output occurs because the `sound()` method is overridden in both the `Cat` and `Cow` subclasses. When these methods are called on their respective objects, the overridden versions execute, producing the expected “Meow” for the `Cat` object and “Moo” for the `Cow` object.

6.6 Practical Exercise: Combining Concepts

Let’s put everything together in a mini-project. Create a class hierarchy that models a simple library system. Use a base class `Item` with subclasses `Book` and `DVD`. Include methods for checking in and checking out items.

Expected Outcome: Demonstrate creating objects of both `Book` and `DVD`, checking them in and out, and displaying their status.

Sample mini-project:

```
// Base class for library items
abstract class Item {
    String title;
    boolean isCheckedOut;

    public Item(String title) {
        this.title = title;
        this.isCheckedOut = false;
    }
```

```
    // Method to check out an item
    public void checkOut() {
        if (!isCheckedOut) {
            isCheckedOut = true;
            System.out.println(title + " has been checked
out.");
        } else {
            System.out.println(title + " is already checked
out.");
        }
    }

    // Method to check in an item
    public void checkIn() {
        if (isCheckedOut) {
            isCheckedOut = false;
            System.out.println(title + " has been checked
in.");
        } else {
            System.out.println(title + " is already checked
in.");
        }
    }

    // Display the status of the item
    public void displayStatus() {
        System.out.println(title + " is " + (isCheckedOut ?
"checked out" : "available") + ".");
    }
}

// Subclass for Books
class Book extends Item {
    String author;

    public Book(String title, String author) {
        super(title);
        this.author = author;
    }
}
```

```
// Subclass for DVDs
class DVD extends Item {
    String director;

    public DVD(String title, String director) {
        super(title);
        this.director = director;
    }
}

// Test class to demonstrate the functionality
public class LibrarySystem {
    public static void main(String[] args) {
        // Creating a book and a DVD
        Book book = new Book("The Great Gatsby", "F. Scott
Fitzgerald");
        DVD dvd = new DVD("Inception", "Christopher Nolan");

        // Checking out and displaying status
        book.checkOut();
        dvd.checkOut();
        book.displayStatus();
        dvd.displayStatus();

        // Checking in and displaying status
        book.checkIn();
        dvd.checkIn();
        book.displayStatus();
        dvd.displayStatus();
    }
}
```

Expected Output:

```
The Great Gatsby has been checked out.
Inception has been checked out.
The Great Gatsby is checked out.
Inception is checked out.
The Great Gatsby has been checked in.
Inception has been checked in.
The Great Gatsby is available.
Inception is available.
```

This above sequence represents the series of actions performed on the `Book` and `DVD` objects: they are first checked out (which marks them as not available), and then checked back in (which marks them as available again), with their status displayed after each action.

Expected Outcome:
When you run the `LibrarySystem` class, it will demonstrate creating objects of both `Book` and `DVD`, checking them in and out, and displaying their status. The console output will indicate the status changes as the items are checked out and checked in.

Explanation for the Mini-Project
This mini-project focuses on modeling a simple library system using the concepts of object-oriented programming (OOP) in Java. This involves understanding and implementing classes, objects, inheritance, and methods to represent and manage a library system. Here's a detailed explanation of how this project can be structured and implemented:

1. Base Class: `Item`

The foundation of the library system is the `Item` class. This class serves as a base class for all items that can be found in a library, including books, DVDs, journals, etc. It contains common attributes that all items share, such as `title`, `author`, and `uniqueID`. Additionally, it includes methods for checking in and checking out items, which can change the status of the item (e.g., available, checked out).

Attributes:

- `title`: The title of the library item.
- `author`: The author or creator of the item.
- `uniqueID`: A unique identifier for each item in the library.

Methods:

- `checkIn()`: Marks the item as available in the library.
- `checkOut()`: Marks the item as checked out and not currently available.

2. Subclasses: `Book` and `DVD`

To represent specific types of library items, you create subclasses that extend the `Item` class. Each subclass can have additional attributes specific to its type. For example:

Book Class:

- Inherits from `Item`.
- May include additional attributes such as `genre`, `publisher`, or `ISBN number`.

DVD Class:

- Inherits from `Item`.
- May include attributes like `duration`, `director`, or `rating`.

These subclasses inherit common attributes and methods from the `Item` class but can also have their unique behaviors and properties.

3. Methods for Managing Library Items

Within each subclass, you can override inherited methods or add new methods to handle behaviors specific to the item type. For instance, you might override the `checkOut()` method in the `DVD` class to include age verification due to rating restrictions.

4. Demonstrating Functionality

To demonstrate the functionality of the library system, you might create a simple driver program (`LibrarySystemDemo`) where you:

- Instantiate objects of the Book and DVD classes.
- Call the `checkIn()` and `checkOut()` methods on these objects.
- Print the status of items to show whether they are available or checked out.

5. Enhancements and Considerations

As enhancements, consider adding features like due dates for checked-out items, tracking who has checked out an item, or implementing fines for late returns. You might also implement a catalog system to search for items by various attributes (title, author, genre, etc.).

Mini-Project Structure:

This mini-project exemplifies key OOP concepts such as inheritance (with `Book` and `DVD` inheriting from `Item`), polymorphism (via method overriding), encapsulation (using private attributes with public getters and setters), and object interaction (checking in and checking out items).

By building this simple library system, beginners can practice and understand how Java's OOP features can be used to model real-world scenarios, laying a foundation for more complex software development projects.

6.7 Check Your Understanding

1. **What is the purpose of a method in Java?**
   A. To execute a specific task or action when called.
   B. To store data.
   C. To define a new data type.
   D. To create a loop.

2. **How do you create an object from a class in Java?**
   A. `ClassName ObjectName;`
   B. `new ClassName();`
   C. `ClassName ObjectName = new ClassName();`
   D. `ClassName();`

3. **What is inheritance in Java?**
   A. The process of increasing the size of an array.
   B. A feature that allows a class to inherit properties and methods from another class.
   C. The act of importing packages.
   D. Creating arrays from objects.

4. **What does the keyword super represent in Java?**
   A. It refers to the superclass's constructor.
   B. It represents the currently executing object.
   C. It is used to call superclass methods from the subclass.
   D. Both A and C.

5. **Which of the following statements is true about polymorphism in Java?**
   A. It allows methods to perform different operations based on the object that is invoking
   the method.
   B. It restricts methods from being reused.
   C. It only applies to static methods.
   D. It prevents classes from inheriting from more than one superclass.

Answers:

1. A-The purpose of a method in Java is to execute a specific task or action when it is called.
2. C - An object is created from a class in Java using the syntax `ClassName ObjectName = new ClassName();`.

3. B - Inheritance is a feature in Java that allows a class to inherit properties and methods from another class.
4. D - The keyword `super` is used both to refer to the superclass's constructor and to call superclass methods from the subclass.
5. A - Polymorphism allows methods to perform different operations based on the object that is invoking the method, enabling the same method to behave differently based on the context in which it is called.

Summary of Key Concepts

Chapter 6 delves into the core principles of Object-Oriented Programming (OOP) in Java, focusing on objects, classes, inheritance, and polymorphism. These concepts are fundamental to Java programming and provide a framework for structuring programs in a way that is both efficient and scalable.

Objects and Classes: At the heart of Java's OOP paradigm are objects and classes. Objects are the building blocks of Java applications. They are instances of classes and encapsulate both state (attributes) and behavior (methods) specific to the entity they represent. Classes, on the other hand, serve as blueprints for creating objects. They define the structure and capabilities that their objects will have. Understanding the relationship between classes and objects is crucial for modeling real-world scenarios within a program.

Inheritance: Inheritance is a mechanism that allows a class to inherit properties and methods from another class, referred to as the parent or superclass. This feature promotes code reuse and establishes a hierarchical classification of classes. Inheritance simplifies code management by allowing developers to create new classes that build upon existing functionality without having to rewrite code from scratch.

Polymorphism: Polymorphism enables objects to perform actions in multiple ways. In Java, this means that a single method name can perform different functions depending on the object that invokes it. This capability is key to implementing method overriding, where a subclass provides a specific implementation of a method already defined in its superclass. Polymorphism enhances flexibility and simplifies code maintenance by allowing programs to handle different data types and perform corresponding operations through a unified interface.

Practical Application: To solidify understanding of these concepts, the chapter introduces a mini-project that integrates objects, classes, inheritance, and polymorphism. This hands-on approach allows learners to apply theoretical knowledge to practical scenarios, reinforcing the importance of OOP principles in building robust and scalable Java applications.

Summary: Chapter 6 equips Java beginners with a deep understanding of OOP principles, emphasizing the creation and manipulation of objects and classes, the hierarchical organization of classes through inheritance, and the flexible behavior of objects via polymorphism. By mastering these concepts, developers can design programs that are modular, extensible, and easy to maintain. The inclusion of a practical application further cements the relevance of these principles in real-world programming, preparing learners to tackle complex development challenges with confidence.

Remember, practice is key to mastering Java programming. Try creating your own classes, experimenting with inheritance, and polymorphism to see what you can build! Next, we'll dive into Java operators and how they work in programming.

Chapter 7: Using Operators

In the world of Java, operators are the “unsung heroes” that help to make sure things are literally operating properly. This chapter covers operators in Java and how they can be used in programs. Java operators are essential tools that allow you to perform various operations on variables and values. This chapter covers the broad categories of operators available in Java, providing beginners with a foundation to write more complex and dynamic programs.

7.1 Arithmetic Operators

Arithmetic operators perform basic mathematical operations. Here’s a simple example to demonstrate these operators:

```
public class ArithmeticDemo {
    public static void main(String[] args) {
        int a = 15, b = 5;
        System.out.println(“Addition: ” + (a + b));
        System.out.println(“Subtraction: ” + (a - b));
        System.out.println(“Multiplication: ” + (a * b));
        System.out.println(“Division: ” + (a / b));
        System.out.println(“Modulus: ” + (a % b));
    }
}
```

Expected Output

```
Addition: 20
Subtraction: 10
Multiplication: 75
Division: 3
Modulus: 0
```

Exercise 7.1:

Create a program that calculates the area of a rectangle with length 7 and width 4 using arithmetic operators.

```
public class RectangleArea {
    public static void main(String[] args) {
        // Assigning values to length and width
        int length = 7;
        int width = 4;

        // Calculating the area of the rectangle
        int area = length * width;

        // Displaying the area
        System.out.println("The area of a rectangle with length
" + length + " and width " + width + " is: " + area);
    }
}
```

Sample Input:	Expected Output:
`Length = 7` `Width = 4`	`The area of a rectangle with length 7 and width 4 is: 28`

7.2 Assignment Operators

Assignment operators assign values to variables. Here's a basic example:

```
public class AssignmentDemo {
    public static void main(String[] args) {
        int x = 10;
        x += 5; // Equivalent to x = x + 5
        System.out.println("Updated x: " + x);
    }
}
```

Expected Output:

```
Updated x: 15
```

Exercise 7.2:

Create a program that calculates the final price after a 10% discount and a 5% tax on an original price of 100.

```
public class FinalPriceCalculator {
    public static void main(String[] args) {
        // Original price of the item
        double originalPrice = 100.0;

        // Discount rate (10%)
        double discountRate = 0.10;

        // Tax rate (5%)
        double taxRate = 0.05;

        // Calculating the price after discount
        double priceAfterDiscount = originalPrice -
(originalPrice * discountRate);

        // Calculating the final price after adding tax
        double finalPrice = priceAfterDiscount +
(priceAfterDiscount * taxRate);

        // Displaying the final price
        System.out.println("The final price after a 10% discount
and 5% tax on an original price of $" + originalPrice + " is:
$" + finalPrice);
    }
}
```

Expected Output

```
The final price after a 10% discount and 5% tax on an original
price of $100.0 is: $94.5
```

7.3 Ternary Operator

The ternary operator is a one-line replacement for the if-then-else statement. Here's how it works:

```
public class TernaryDemo {
    public static void main(String[] args) {
        int age = 18;
        String eligibility = (age >= 18) ? "Eligible to vote" :
"Not eligible to vote";
        System.out.println(eligibility);
    }
}
```

Expected Output

```
Eligible to vote
```

Exercise 7.3:
Create a program that uses the ternary operator to find the greater of two numbers.

```
public class GreaterNumberFinder {
    public static void main(String[] args) {
        // Define two numbers
        int number1 = 10;
        int number2 = 20;

        // Use the ternary operator to find the greater number
        int greaterNumber = (number1 > number2) ? number1 :
number2;

        // Display the result
        System.out.println("The greater number between " +
number1 + " and " + number2 + " is: " + greaterNumber);
    }
}
```

This program defines two numbers, `number1` and `number2`, and then uses the ternary operator to check which one is greater. It then prints out the greater number. If you run this program, the **Expected Output** will be:

```
The greater number between 10 and 20 is: 20
```

7.4 Logical Operators

Logical operators (`&&`, `||`) are used to combine multiple conditions. Here's a quick example:

```
public class LogicalDemo {
    public static void main(String[] args) {
        boolean isAdult = true;
        boolean hasVoterID = false;
        System.out.println("Can vote: " + (isAdult &&
hasVoterID));
    }
}
```

Expected Output

```
Can vote: false
```

Exercise 7.4:

Create a program that checks if a number is positive and even uses logical operators.

```
public class CheckPositiveAndEven {
    public static void main(String[] args) {
        // Sample input number
        int number = 24;

        // Check if the number is positive and even
        if(number > 0 && number % 2 == 0) {
            System.out.println("The number " + number + " is
positive and even.");
        } else {
            System.out.println("The number " + number + " is
not both positive and even.");
        }
    }
}
```

For this program, the sample input is the number 24. Given this input, the **Expected Output** would be:

```
The number 24 is positive and even.
```

7.5 Bitwise Operators

Bitwise operators perform operations on individual bits. Here's an example demonstrating bitwise AND:

```
public class BitwiseDemo {
    public static void main(String[] args) {
        int a = 5; // 0101 in binary
        int b = 3; // 0011 in binary
        System.out.println("a & b: " + (a & b));
    }
}
```

Expected Output

```
a & b: 1
```

Exercise 7.5:
Write a program that uses bitwise operators to multiply and divide a number by 2.

```
public class BitwiseMultiplyDivide {
    public static void main(String[] args) {
        // Sample input number
        int number = 8;

        // Multiply the number by 2 using bitwise left shift
        int multiplyByTwo = number << 1;

        // Divide the number by 2 using bitwise right shift
        int divideByTwo = number >> 1;

        // Display the results
        System.out.println("Original number: " + number);
        System.out.println("After multiplication by 2: " +
multiplyByTwo);
        System.out.println("After division by 2: " +
divideByTwo);
    }
}
```

For this program, the sample input is the number 8. Given this input, the expected output would be:

```
Original number: 8
After multiplication by 2: 16
After division by 2: 4
```

7.6 Check Your Understanding

1. **Basic Arithmetic Operators: What will be the result of the expression** 8 % 3?
2. **Assignment Operators: Given** `int x = 5; x += 3;`**, what is the final value of** `x`?
3. **Ternary Operator: What does the expression** `int result = (10 > 5) ? 1 : 0;` **evaluate to?**
4. **Logical Operators: Evaluate the expression** `false || true && false`. **What is the result?**
5. **Bitwise Operators: What is the result of** `4 & 5` **using bitwise AND operator?**

6. **Shift Operators: What does `15 >> 2` evaluate to?**
7. **Combining Operators: Given `int x = 5; int y = 10;`, what does `(x * 2 + y) / 5` evaluate to?**
8. **Unary Operators: What is the value of x after evaluating `int x = 10; ++x;`?**
9. **Relational Operators: Given `int a = 5, b = 10;`, is `a >= b` true or false?**
10. **Operator Precedence: What is the result of the expression `3 + 4 * 5` and why?**

Answers:

1. 2 (Remainder of 8 divided by 3 is 2)
2. 8 (`x` is incremented by 3, making it 8)
3. 1 (The condition `10 > 5` is true, so it evaluates to 1)
4. False (`true && false` is `false`, then `false || false` is `false`)
5. 4 (Binary of 4 is `100` and 5 is `101`, AND operation gives `100` which is 4)
6. 3 (Right shift by 2 divides the number by 2^2 = 4, so 15 / 4 = 3)
7. 6 (`(5 * 2 + 10) / 5` equals `20 / 5` which equals 4)
8. 11 (`++x` increments `x` before it's used, making it 11)
9. False (`5` is not greater than or equal to `10`)
10. 23 (Multiplication has higher precedence than addition, so `4 * 5` is evaluated first to give 20, then `3 + 20` equals 23)

7.7 Fun Exercises for Chapter 7:

Each of these exercises is designed to reinforce your understanding of Java operators in a fun and practical context, making it easier to apply these concepts in real-world programming challenges.

1. Arithmetic Puzzle: Create a program that solves the puzzle: "What is the result of multiplying the sum of 11 and 5 by the difference of 20 and 12?"

2. Assignment Adventure: Make a game that starts with a number of gold coins. The player finds more coins or spends some, updating the total using assignment operators.

3. Magical Number: Use the ternary operator to check if a number is magical (divisible by 3 and 5). If so, print "Magic Number"; otherwise, print "Ordinary Number".

1. Sample Program

```
public class ArithmeticPuzzle {
    public static void main(String[] args) {
        // Calculate the sum of 11 and 5
        int sum = 11 + 5;

        // Calculate the difference of 20 and 12
        int difference = 20 - 12;

        // Multiply the sum by the difference
        int result = sum * difference;

        // Display the result
        System.out.println("The result of multiplying the sum
of 11 and 5 by the difference of 20 and 12 is: " + result);
    }
}
```

```
The result of multiplying the sum of 11 and 5 by the difference
of 20 and 12 is: 128
```

2. Sample Program

Game Design:

Starting Gold: The player starts with a predefined number of gold coins.

Finding Gold: The player finds gold, adding to their total.

Spending Gold: The player spends gold, subtracting from their total.

Display Total: The current total gold is displayed after each action.

```
import java.util.Scanner;

public class GoldGame {
    public static void main(String[] args) {
        int goldCoins = 50; // Starting gold
        Scanner scanner = new Scanner(System.in);

        System.out.println("Welcome to the Gold Game!");
        System.out.println("You start with " + goldCoins + "
gold coins.");
```

```
while (true) {
        System.out.println("\nWhat would you like to do?");
        System.out.println("1. Find gold");
        System.out.println("2. Spend gold");
        System.out.println("3. Check gold");
        System.out.println("4. Exit");

        System.out.print("Enter your choice (1-4): ");
        int choice = scanner.nextInt();

        switch (choice) {
            case 1: // Find gold
                System.out.print("How much gold did you find? ");
                int found = scanner.nextInt();
                goldCoins += found; // Using assignment operator
                System.out.println("You found " + found + " gold
                coins.");
                break;
            case 2: // Spend gold
                System.out.print("How much gold do you want to
                spend? ");
                int spent = scanner.nextInt();
                if (spent <= goldCoins) {
                    goldCoins -= spent; // Using assignment
                    operator
                    System.out.println("You spent " + spent + "
                    gold coins.");
                } else {
                    System.out.println("You don't have enough
                    gold!");
                }
                break;
            case 3: // Check gold
                System.out.println("You currently have " +
                goldCoins + " gold coins.");
                break;
```

```
                case 4: // Exit
                    System.out.println("Exiting the game. Final gold
                    count: " + goldCoins);
                    return;
                default:
                    System.out.println("Invalid choice. Please choose
                    again.");
                    break;
            }
        }
    }
}
```

```
Sample Input and Output
Welcome to the Gold Game!
You start with 50 gold coins.

What would you like to do?
1. Find gold
2. Spend gold
3. Check gold
4. Exit
Enter your choice (1-4): 1
How much gold did you find? 20
You found 20 gold coins.

What would you like to do?
1. Find gold
2. Spend gold
3. Check gold
4. Exit
Enter your choice (1-4): 2
How much gold do you want to spend? 30
You spent 30 gold coins.

What would you like to do?
1. Find gold
2. Spend gold
3. Check gold
4. Exit
Enter your choice (1-4): 3
You currently have 40 gold coins.
```

```
What would you like to do?
1. Find gold
2. Spend gold
3. Check gold
4. Exit
Enter your choice (1-4): 4
Exiting the game. Final gold count: 40
```

3. Sample program

```
import java.util.Scanner;

public class MagicNumberChecker {
    public static void main(String[] args) {
        Scanner scanner = new Scanner(System.in);
        System.out.print("Enter a number: ");
        int number = scanner.nextInt();

        String result = (number % 3 == 0 && number % 5 == 0) ?
"Magic Number" : "Ordinary Number";
        System.out.println(result);
    }
}
```

Sample Input and Output:

```
Enter a number: 15
Output: Magic Number

Enter a number: 30
Output: Magic Number

Enter a number: 14
Output: Ordinary Number
```

Summary of Key Concepts

Chapter 7 of our beginner-friendly guide to Java programming introduced the concept of operators, which are symbols that tell the compiler to perform specific mathematical or logical manipulations. This chapter is essential for understanding how to control the flow of a Java program and manipulate data effectively. Here's a summary of the key concepts and the types of operators covered:

7.1 Arithmetic Operators

- Purpose: Perform basic mathematical operations.
- Key Operators: + (addition), - (subtraction), * (multiplication), / (division), and % (modulus).
- Example Use: Calculating the area of a rectangle or converting temperature units.

7.2 Assignment Operators

- Purpose: Assign values to variables.
- Key Operators: = (simple assignment), += (add and assign), -=, *=, /=, and %= for various arithmetic assignments.
- Example Use: Updating the value of a variable, like incrementing a score in a game.

7.3 Ternary Operator

- Purpose: Simplify an if-then-else statement into a single line.
- Syntax: condition ? expressionIfTrue : expressionIfFalse.
- Example Use: Determining eligibility for voting based on age.

7.4 Logical Operators

- Purpose: Combine multiple boolean expressions.
- Key Operators: && (logical AND), || (logical OR), and ! (logical NOT).
- Example Use: Checking if a user is eligible for a discount based on multiple conditions.

7.5 Bitwise Operators

- Purpose: Operate on individual bits of integer types.
- Key Operators: & (AND), | (OR), ^ (XOR), ~ (NOT), << (left shift), >> (right shift), and >>> (unsigned right shift).
- Example Use: Manipulating color values in graphics programming or performing quick math operations of multiplication or division by powers of 2.

This chapter laid the groundwork for understanding how operators are used to perform various operations in Java programming. From basic arithmetic to complex bitwise manipulations, operators are fundamental to controlling the flow and logic of a program. Exercises provided practical applications of these concepts, reinforcing learning and demonstrating how operators can be used in real-world scenarios.

Moving forward, learners are encouraged to experiment with these operators in their Java programs, exploring the various ways they can be combined to achieve desired outcomes and solve problems efficiently.

Key Concepts:

- Operators Enable Data Manipulation: Java operators allow for the manipulation of variables and values, enabling complex computations and logical conditions within a program.
- Choice of Operator Affects Efficiency: Selecting the appropriate operator, such as using shift operators for certain multiplications or divisions, can improve a program's efficiency.
- Operators Facilitate Decision Making: Through logical and relational operators, programs can make decisions and execute different code paths based on certain conditions.

Having explored the diverse operators available in Java, you're now equipped to craft programs capable of executing a variety of mathematical operations with ease. This foundational understanding sets the stage for our next journey into the realm of Java programming where we'll delve into the efficient management of data through the use of arrays and collections. Stay tuned as we unravel the intricacies of organizing and manipulating data, enhancing both the functionality and sophistication of your Java applications.

Chapter 8: Simplified Data Management with Arrays and Collections for Beginners

In the realm of Java programming, managing multiple data elements efficiently is paramount. This chapter demystifies arrays and collections, empowering beginners to handle groups of data with ease.

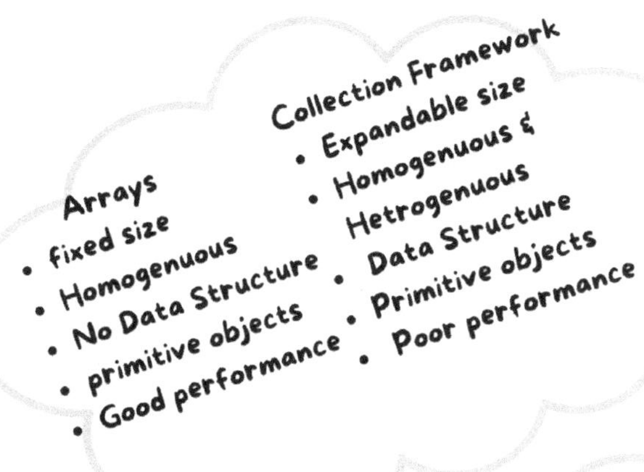

8.1 Introduction to Arrays

8.1.1 What is an Array?

An array in Java is a powerful tool for storing a series of elements of the same type. Think of it as a container where you can store items of the same kind, neatly indexed starting from zero. Whether it's a bunch of integers or strings, arrays keep them organized and easily accessible.

8.1.2 Creating and Using Arrays

Creating an array is straightforward. You decide on the type of data it will hold and its size, then Java carves out a space in memory for it. Here's how you can make an array of integers:

```
int[] numbers = new int[5]; // An array for 5 integers
```

To fill this array with data:

```
numbers[0] = 10; // Assigning the first element
```

Exercise 8.1: Array Basics

Try It Out: Create an integer array named `ages` and fill it with the ages 10, 15, 20, 25, and 30. Print out the third age in the list.

Sample Answer:

```
int[] ages = {10, 15, 20, 25, 30};
System.out.println("The third age is: " + ages[2]);
```

Expected Output:

```
numbers[0] = 10; // Assigning the first element
```

Fun Exercise 8.1: Dynamic Guest List

Objective: Create a program that manages a dynamic guest list for an event using an ArrayList. Allow adding and removing guests by name and display the updated list after each operation.

Sample program:

This Java program allows users to dynamically manage a guest list for an event using an `ArrayList`. Users can add and remove guests by name and display the current guest list. The program continues running until the user types "exit".

```
import java.util.ArrayList;
import java.util.Scanner;

public class DynamicGuestList {
    public static void main(String[] args) {
        ArrayList<String> guestList = new ArrayList<>();
        Scanner scanner = new Scanner(System.in);
        String input = "";
        System.out.println("Dynamic Guest List Manager");

        while (!input.equalsIgnoreCase("exit")) {
            System.out.println("\nChoose an operation:");
            System.out.println("1: Add Guest");
            System.out.println("2: Remove Guest");
            System.out.println("3: Display Guest List");
            System.out.println("Type 'exit' to quit");

            input = scanner.nextLine();

            switch (input) {
                case "1":
                    System.out.println("Enter guest's name to add:");
                    String nameToAdd = scanner.nextLine();
                    guestList.add(nameToAdd);
                    System.out.println(nameToAdd + " has been added to the guest list.");
                    break;
                case "2":
                    System.out.println("Enter guest's name to remove:");
                    String nameToRemove = scanner.nextLine();
                    if (guestList.remove(nameToRemove)) {
                        System.out.println(nameToRemove + " has been removed from the guest
list.");
                    } else {
                        System.out.println(nameToRemove + " was not found in the guest list.");
                    }
                    break;
                case "3":
                    System.out.println("Current Guest List:");
                    for (String guest : guestList) {
                        System.out.println(guest);
                    }
                    break;
                default:
                    if (!input.equalsIgnoreCase("exit")) {
                        System.out.println("Invalid input. Please try again.");
                    }
                    break;
            }
        }
        System.out.println("Goodbye!");
    }
}
```

Sample Input:	Expected Output:
1 John 2 Jane 3 exit	Dynamic Guest List Manager Choose an operation: 1: Add Guest 2: Remove Guest 3: Display Guest List Type 'exit' to quit Enter guest's name to add: John John has been added to the guest list. Choose an operation: 1: Add Guest 2: Remove Guest 3: Display Guest List Type 'exit' to quit Enter guest's name to remove: Jane Jane was not found in the guest list. Choose an operation: 1: Add Guest 2: Remove Guest 3: Display Guest List Type 'exit' to quit Current Guest List: John Choose an operation: 1: Add Guest 2: Remove Guest 3: Display Guest List Type 'exit' to quit Goodbye!

8.2 Dive into Collections

8.2.1 Understanding Collections

Collections come to the rescue in situations where arrays have limitations or drawbacks that make them less suitable for certain tasks. Specifically, the situations refer to the fixed size of arrays, which means they cannot easily accommodate changes in the number of elements they hold. Collections offer a dynamic solution, allowing you to add, remove, and manipulate groups of objects more flexibly compared to arrays.

8.2.2 Types of Collections

- ArrayList: Similar to a dynamic array, it expands as you add elements.
- HashSet: Great for storing unique elements without any order.
- LinkedList: Each element links to its predecessor and successor, making insertions and deletions super efficient.

Exercise 8.2: Fun with Collections

Challenge: Create an ArrayList named colors and add “Red”, “Blue”, and “Green”. Print the entire list.

Sample Code:

```
ArrayList<String> colors = new ArrayList<>();
colors.add("Red");
colors.add("Blue");
colors.add("Green");
System.out.println(colors);
```

Expected Output:

```
[Red, Blue, Green]
```

Fun Exercise 8.2: Unique Number Collection

Objective: Write a program that collects numbers in a HashSet to ensure all numbers are unique. Allow the user to add numbers and then display the unique numbers in no particular order.

This program prompts the user to enter numbers one by one. If the user inputs something that is not a number or types "done," the program will either warn about the invalid input or proceed to display all unique numbers added so far, thanks to the properties of `HashSet` which automatically ensures uniqueness.

Instructions:

1. Create a `HashSet` to store integers.
2. Add functionality to insert numbers into the set.
3. Display the unique numbers stored in the set after all additions.
4. Demonstrate that duplicates are automatically removed.

Sample Program

```
import java.util.HashSet;
import java.util.Scanner;
import java.util.Set;

public class UniqueNumbersCollector {
    public static void main(String[] args) {
        Set<Integer> uniqueNumbers = new HashSet<>();
        Scanner scanner = new Scanner(System.in);
        String input = "";

        System.out.println("Unique Numbers Collector");
        System.out.println("Enter numbers to add to the set.
Type 'done' to finish and display unique numbers.");

        while (!input.equalsIgnoreCase("done")) {
            System.out.print("Enter a number (or 'done' to
finish): ");
            input = scanner.nextLine();

            if (input.equalsIgnoreCase("done")) {
                break;
            }
```

```
            try {
                int number = Integer.parseInt(input);
                if (uniqueNumbers.add(number)) {
                    System.out.println(number + " added.");
                } else {
                    System.out.println(number + " is already in
the set and was not added.");
                }
            } catch (NumberFormatException e) {
                System.out.println("Invalid input. Please enter
a valid number.");
            }
        }

        System.out.println("\nUnique numbers in no particular
order:");
        for (int number : uniqueNumbers) {
            System.out.println(number);
        }
    }
}
```

Sample Input:	Expected Output:

`Add: 5`
`Add: 3`
`Add: 5`
`Add: 8`
	`Unique Numbers: 3, 5, 8`

8.3 Manipulating Data with Arrays and Collections

8.3.1 Array Manipulation

Arrays facilitate direct access and modification of elements via their index. Iterating through arrays enables batch operations such as sorting or aggregating elements.

8.3.2 Collection Manipulation

Collections offer a rich set of methods for data manipulation, including adding, removing, and searching elements. The flexibility and power of collections make managing data easier and more intuitive.

Exercise 8.3: Array and Collection Manipulation

Task: Create an ArrayList named `numbers` and add the first five positive integers. Then, remove the number "3" and print the new list.

Sample Solution:

```
ArrayList<Integer> numbers = new ArrayList<>();
numbers.add(1);
numbers.add(2);
numbers.add(3);
numbers.add(4);
numbers.add(5);
numbers.remove(new Integer(3));
System.out.println(numbers);
```

Expected Output: `[1, 2, 4, 5]`

Fun Exercise 8.3: Task Organizer

Objective: Develop a program that uses a LinkedList to manage tasks in a to-do list. Include options to add a task, remove a task by index, and display the current list of tasks.

This program allows users to manage a to-do list by adding tasks, removing tasks by index, and viewing the current list of tasks. The to-do list is implemented using a `LinkedList`, offering efficient insertion and removal operations. The program continues running until the user types "exit."

Instructions:

1. Use a `LinkedList` to keep track of tasks.
2. Implement methods for adding tasks to the end of the list and removing tasks by their position in the list.
3. After each operation, print the list of current tasks.
4. Validate the removal operation to ensure it handles invalid indices gracefully.

Sample Program:

```
import java.util.LinkedList;
import java.util.Scanner;

public class ToDoListManager {
    public static void main(String[] args) {
        LinkedList<String> toDoList = new LinkedList<>();
        Scanner scanner = new Scanner(System.in);
        String input = "";
        System.out.println("To-Do List Manager");

        while (!input.equalsIgnoreCase("exit")) {
            System.out.println("\nChoose an operation:");
            System.out.println("1: Add Task");
            System.out.println("2: Remove Task");
            System.out.println("3: Display To-Do List");
            System.out.println("Type 'exit' to quit");

            input = scanner.nextLine();

            switch (input) {
                case "1":
                    System.out.println("Enter task to add:");
                    String taskToAdd = scanner.nextLine();
                    toDoList.add(taskToAdd);
                    System.out.println("'" + taskToAdd + "' has 
been added to your to-do list.");
                    break;
                case "2":
                    System.out.println("Enter task index to 
remove (starting from 0):");
                    int indexToRemove;
                    try {
                        indexToRemove = Integer.
parseInt(scanner.nextLine());
                        if (indexToRemove >= 0 && indexToRemove 
< toDoList.size()) {
                            String removedTask = toDoList.
remove(indexToRemove);
```

```
                            System.out.println("'" +
removedTask + "' has been removed from your to-do list.");
                        } else {
                            System.out.println("Invalid index.
Please try again.");
                        }
                    } catch (NumberFormatException e) {
                        System.out.println("Please enter a
valid number.");
                    }
                    break;
                case "3":
                    System.out.println("Current To-Do List:");
                    for (int i = 0; i < toDoList.size(); i++) {
                        System.out.println(i + ": " + toDoList.
get(i));
                    }
                    break;
                default:
                    if (!input.equalsIgnoreCase("exit")) {
                        System.out.println("Invalid input.
Please try again.");
                    }
                    break;
            }
        }
        System.out.println("Goodbye!");
    }
}
```

Sample Input:	Expected Output:
Add: Finish homework Add: Go grocery shopping Remove: 0 (index) Add: Call mom	Tasks: Finish homework, Go grocery shopping Tasks: Go grocery shopping Tasks: Go grocery shopping, Call mom

8.4 Check Your Understanding

1. What's the starting index of an array in Java?
2. How does an ArrayList differ from a regular array?

3. How can you remove an element from an ArrayList?
4. Why would you choose a HashSet over an ArrayList?
5. Can you store different types of data in an array? Why or why not?

Answers:

1. The starting index of an array in Java is 0. This means the first element of any array is accessed with the index 0.
2. An ArrayList is dynamic, meaning it can grow or shrink in size as elements are added or removed, offering more flexibility than a regular array, which has a fixed size once it's created.
3. You can remove an element from an ArrayList using the `.remove()` method. You can pass either the index of the element you want to remove or the element itself if you're working with an ArrayList of objects. For example, `numbers.remove(2);` or `colors.remove("Blue");`.
4. You would choose a HashSet over an ArrayList when you need to ensure that all elements are unique and you don't care about the order of elements. A HashSet does not allow duplicate values and does not maintain the order of its elements, unlike an ArrayList.
5. No, you cannot store different types of data in a single array in Java. An array is a homogeneous data structure, meaning it can only store elements of the same data type. This restriction ensures type safety and efficiency in array operations. However, you can store objects of different classes in an array of type `Object`, since all classes in Java inherit from the `Object` class, but this approach is not type-safe and is generally not recommended.

Summary of Key Concepts

Chapter 8 delves into managing data with Arrays and Collections in Java, providing the tools needed to organize and manipulate groups of elements efficiently. Here's a detailed summary:

8.1 Arrays

- Definition and Importance: Arrays store multiple elements of the same data type in contiguous memory locations. They simplify handling large data sets by allowing operations such as retrieval and sorting more efficiently than with individual variables.
- Creation and Initialization: Arrays can be declared and initialized in

a single statement or in separate statements. Their size, defined at creation, cannot be changed, posing a limitation for dynamic data handling.

- Types of Arrays: Java supports single-dimensional and multi-dimensional arrays. Multi-dimensional arrays, useful for grid-like data structures, can be initialized with or without specifying values for each element.

8.2 Collections

- Collection vs. Array: Collections provide enhanced flexibility for managing groups of objects compared to arrays. Unlike arrays, collections can adapt their size dynamically and offer diverse data structures like lists, sets, and queues to suit varying requirements.
- Framework Overview: The collection framework furnishes a unified structure for storing and handling groups of objects. It encompasses interfaces such as List, Set, and Queue, along with classes of ArrayList, HashSet, and LinkedList, which implement these interfaces.
- Demonstrated Examples: The chapter illustrates the usage of ArrayList and HashSet through practical examples. ArrayList facilitates dynamic storage and manipulation of elements in ordered collections capable of containing duplicates. Conversely, HashSet stores unique elements without a specified ordering.

8.3 Working with Collections

- Operations: Common operations include adding, removing, and accessing elements. The ArrayList class, for instance, supports dynamic arrays that can grow as needed.
- Iterators: Iterators are used to cycle through collections, allowing for element access and modification during iteration. The iterator method offers a standardized way to traverse collections.

Check Your Understanding

- The chapter wraps up with hands-on exercises designed to reinforce comprehension of arrays and collections. These exercises task readers with putting concepts into practice, such as sorting arrays, calculating the sum of array elements, and manipulating collections through diverse operations.

Summary

Chapter 8 equips Java programmers with the necessary understanding to manage data effectively using arrays and collections. By mastering these concepts, developers can handle complex data structures, improve the efficiency of their code, and leverage Java's powerful data manipulation capabilities for robust application development. Through practical examples and exercises, readers are encouraged to explore the flexibility and functionality offered by Java's array and collection frameworks, setting a solid foundation for more advanced data handling and algorithmic challenges.

Chapter 9: Navigating Through Errors and Exceptions in Java

In the realm of programming, smooth sailing isn't always guaranteed. Occasionally, unforeseen circumstances can disrupt your program's flow or even halt its execution. This chapter delves into the nuances of error and exception handling, illuminating strategies for navigating these unforeseen scenarios and ensuring the seamless operation of your Java programs.

9.1 Understanding Errors and Exceptions

Errors: These denote predicaments that transcend your authority, such as when your computer exhausts its memory. They signify grave quandaries typically arising from anomalies in the environment where your program operates, rather than inherent flaws in your code.

Exceptions: These arise during program execution, such as attempting to access a nonexistent file. Unlike errors, you can anticipate and manage exceptions to sustain your program's functionality.

Fun Exercise: Catching a Missing File

- Create a program that tries to read a file that doesn't exist and catch the resulting exception, printing a message, "`Oops! The file doesn't exist.`"

Sample Program: `FileNotFoundException`

```
import java.io.File;
import java.io.FileNotFoundException;
import java.util.Scanner;

public class MissingFileExample {
    public static void main(String[] args) {
        try {
            // Attempting to read a file that doesn't exist
            File file = new File("nonexistentfile.txt");
            Scanner scanner = new Scanner(file);
            while (scanner.hasNextLine()) {
                String line = scanner.nextLine();
                System.out.println(line);
            }
            scanner.close();
        } catch (FileNotFoundException e) {
            // Catching the FileNotFoundException and printing
a message
            System.out.println("Oops! The file doesn't exist.");
        }
    }
}
```

Expected Output: `Oops! The file doesn't exist.`

Explanation: This program demonstrates basic exception handling in Java, specifically handling a `FileNotFoundException` by using a `try-catch` block.

What is a `try-catch` block?

A `try-catch` block in Java is a mechanism for handling exceptions, which are events that disrupt the normal flow of program execution. It allows you to define a block of code to be tested for errors while it is being executed (`try` block) and a block of code to be executed if an error occurs in the try block (`catch` block). This mechanism provides a way to catch and handle exceptions gracefully, preventing the program from crashing and allowing for more robust and error-resistant code.

Structure of a try-catch block:

```
try {
    // Code that might throw an exception
} catch (ExceptionType name) {
    // Code to handle the exception
}
```

- **try block:** Contains the code that might throw an exception. If an exception occurs within this block, execution of the block is stopped, and control is transferred to the corresponding catch block that can handle this type of exception.
- **catch block:** Contains the code to handle the exception thrown by the try block. The catch block specifies the type of exception it can handle in parentheses. If the thrown exception matches the type specified in the catch block (or a superclass of it), the code within the catch block is executed.

Example:

```
try {
    int result = 10 / 0; // This line will throw an
ArithmeticException
} catch (ArithmeticException e) {
    System.out.println("Cannot divide by zero!"); // Handle the
exception
}
```

Explanation: In this example, dividing by zero causes an `ArithmeticException` to be thrown. The `catch` block catches this exception and executes its code, printing "Cannot divide by zero!" to the console, instead of causing the program to crash.

Points to Note:

- A single try block can be followed by multiple catch blocks to handle different types of exceptions separately.
- A `finally` block can also be used after catch blocks to execute code that should run regardless of whether an exception was thrown and caught, such as cleaning up resources like closing file streams or database connections.

- Not all exceptions need to be caught with a try-catch block; some are checked exceptions that must be either caught or declared in the method signature with `throws`, while others are unchecked exceptions (like `RuntimeException` and its subclasses) that the programmer can choose to catch or not.

9.2 Types of Exceptions

Java divides exceptions into two main categories:

- Checked Exceptions: These are the exceptions the compiler checks for at compile time. If your code could cause one of these exceptions, Java insists that you handle it, either by using a `try-catch` block or by declaring the exception with `throws`.
- Unchecked Exceptions (Runtime Exceptions): These occur while your program is running, and they're usually due to bugs in your code, like trying to access an element in an array that doesn't exist.

Fun Exercise: Handling an Array Error

- Create an array and try to access an index that is out of bounds.
- Catch the resulting `ArrayIndexOutOfBoundsException` and print "Oops! `We tried to access a wrong index.`"

Sample Program `ArrayAccessError`

```
public class ArrayAccessError {
    public static void main(String[] args) {
        int[] array = {1, 2, 3, 4, 5}; // An array with 5
elements
        try {
            // Attempt to access an index out of bounds
            System.out.println(array[10]);
        } catch (ArrayIndexOutOfBoundsException e) {
            // Catch the ArrayIndexOutOfBoundsException and
print a custom message
            System.out.println("Oops! We tried to access a
wrong index.");
        }
    }
}
```

Expected Output: `Oops! We tried to access a wrong index.`

Explanation: In this program, an attempt is made to access an element at index 10 of an array that only contains five elements. This operation throws an `ArrayIndexOutOfBoundsException`, which is caught by the `catch` block, printing "We tried to access a wrong index." to the console.

9.3 Exception Handling Techniques

Java provides several keywords for handling exceptions:

- `try-catch`: Encapsulate the code that might throw an exception in a try block, and catch the exception in a catch block.
- `finally`: A block of code that always executes, regardless of whether an exception was thrown or caught.
- `throws`: Used in method signatures to indicate that this method might throw an exception.

Fun Exercise: Safely Dividing Numbers

- Write a method that divides two numbers but could throw an ArithmeticException if you try to divide by zero.
- Use `try-catch` to handle the exception and print "`Cannot divide by zero.`"

Sample Program:

```
public class DivisionExample {

    public static void main(String[] args) {
        divideNumbers(10, 0);
        divideNumbers(10, 2);
    }

    // Method to divide two numbers
    public static void divideNumbers(int numerator, int
denominator) {
        try {
            int result = numerator / denominator;
            System.out.println("Result: " + result);
        } catch (ArithmeticException e) {
            // Handle the ArithmeticException for division by
zero
            System.out.println("Cannot divide by zero.");
        }
    }
}
```

Expected Output: `Cannot divide by zero.`

Explanation: This program defines a `divideNumbers` method that attempts to divide two integers. If the denominator is zero, an `ArithmeticException` is thrown, which is caught by the catch block, printing "Cannot divide by zero." to the console. The `main` method demonstrates using `divideNumbers` with both a valid division and an attempt to divide by zero to trigger the exception handling.

9.4 Custom Exceptions

Sometimes, the standard Java exceptions don't quite fit the error situation in your code. In these cases, you can create your own exceptions.

Fun Exercise: Making Your Own Exception

- Create a custom exception called `MyException` that you throw if a certain condition in your code isn't met.
- Catch your custom exception and print "`MyException occurred.`"

Sample Program:

```
// Define the custom exception
class MyException extends Exception {
    public MyException(String message) {
        super(message);
    }
}

public class CustomExceptionExample {

    public static void main(String[] args) {
        try {
            // Call a method that may throw MyException
            checkCondition(false);
        } catch (MyException e) {
            // Catch and handle MyException
            System.out.println("MyException occurred.");
        }
    }

    // Method that throws MyException based on a condition
    public static void checkCondition(boolean condition) throws
MyException {
```

```
        if (!condition) {
            throw new MyException("Condition not met.");
        }
        System.out.println("Condition met.");
    }
}
```

Expected Output: `MyException occurred.`

Explanation:

- The `MyException` class is a custom exception that extends `Exception` and includes a constructor for passing messages.
- The `checkCondition` method throws a `MyException` if the passed boolean condition is `false`.
- In the `main` method, checkCondition is called with false to deliberately fail the condition, triggering the `MyException`.
- The `catch` block catches `MyException` and prints "MyException occurred." to the console.

Summary of Key Concepts

Errors and exceptions might seem intimidating at first, but they're just Java's way of telling you that something unexpected happened. By understanding and handling these situations, you can make your programs more robust and user-friendly. Chapter 9 equips Java programmers with the understanding and tools necessary to effectively navigate through errors and exceptions. By mastering these concepts, programmers can ensure that their applications are capable of handling unexpected situations gracefully, thereby improving the overall quality and reliability of their code.

Key Concepts

- Proper error and exception handling are fundamental to creating robust, stable, and user-friendly Java applications.
- The distinction between checked and unchecked exceptions helps programmers deal with both foreseeable and unforeseeable issues in their code.
- Employing custom exceptions can significantly enhance the readability and maintainability of exception handling code by allowing for more descriptive error messages and categorization of error types.

Next Step

Congratulations! You've learned how to deal with unexpected events in your Java programs. Next, we'll explore Java's input and output capabilities, allowing your programs to interact with users and external data sources more effectively.

Chapter 10: Java Input and Output (I/O)

Introduction

Java's Input/Output (I/O) capabilities are akin to the enchantment operating behind the scenes, breathing life into your applications. Envision a dialogue with a friend; Java I/O facilitates precisely that, albeit with data! Whether it involves recording your high score in a game, completing a form in an app, or transmitting a message, Java I/O is the driving force. It revolves around ingesting data, such as parsing through a list of beloved songs from a file, and disseminating data, like archiving your latest doodle for future sharing.

To enable this functionality, Java employs streams and files, resembling the conduits and repositories in an intricate plumbing network. Streams emulate flowing water, smoothly transferring data in and out of your programs, bit by bit. They adeptly handle various data types, spanning from text to adorable kitten pictures. Conversely, files act as reservoirs, conserving data for subsequent utilization, similar to maintaining a journal of your escapades within a game. Together, they ensure the seamless flow of data, whether it's materializing on your display, being archived for future reference, or being dispatched into the vast expanse of the internet. Thus, Java I/O assumes the role of a clandestine wizard backstage, ensuring your application converses fluently with the surrounding world.

10.1 Understanding Streams

In the world of Java's I/O, streams are the magical pathways that allow data to flow seamlessly between your program and an external source or destination. Imagine a stream of water in nature; just as water flows from one point to another, data flows through streams from a source to your program or from your program to a destination.

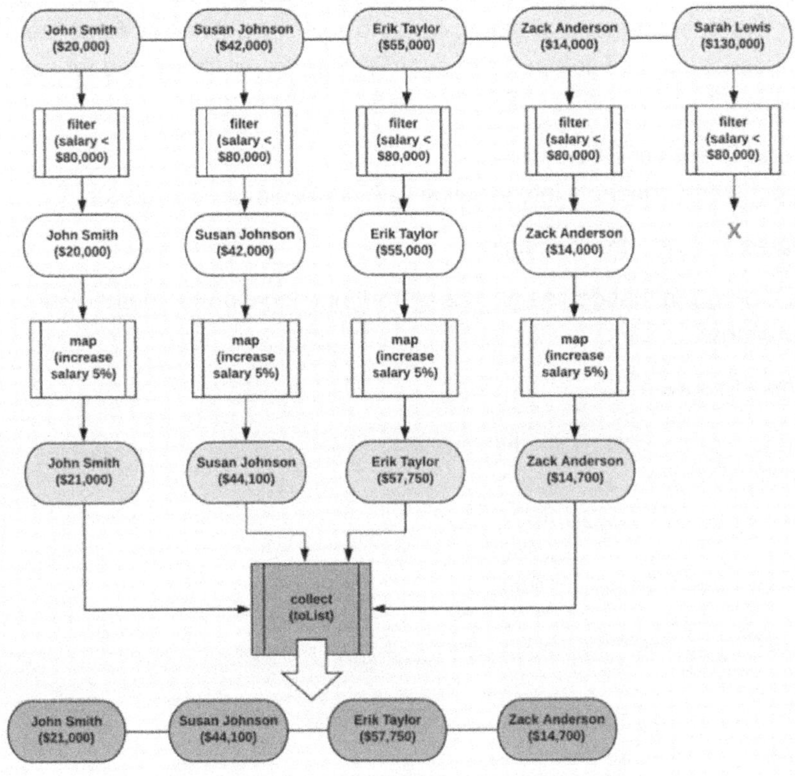

https://theboreddev.com/understanding-java-streams/

Types of Streams

Java cleverly employs two primary categories of streams to manage data: byte streams and character streams.

Byte Streams: These manage data byte by byte, particularly adept at handling raw binary data such as images or music files. Picture it as processing data meticulously, where each minuscule segment represents a byte.

Character Streams: Designed to manage character data effectively, such as the text content in this explanation. They smoothly handle the conversion to and from the local character set, making them ideal for textual files.

Stream Hierarchy

Java organizes these streams into a hierarchical structure, streamlining comprehension and efficient usage. At the apex, abstract classes like

InputStream and OutputStream oversee byte streams, while Reader and Writer oversee character streams. A plethora of specialized streams stem from these, such as FileInputStream or FileReader, each tailored for specific functions.

Fun and Practical Exercises

Let's put these concepts into practice with some simple exercises:

Exercise 1: Byte Stream Magic

Write a program that copies an image from one location to another using byte streams.

Example Program

```
import java.io.FileInputStream;
import java.io.FileOutputStream;
import java.io.IOException;

public class ImageCopier {
    public static void main(String[] args) {
        try (FileInputStream in = new FileInputStream("source.
jpg");
             FileOutputStream out = new
FileOutputStream("destination.jpg")) {
            int bite;
            while ((bite = in.read()) != -1) {
                out.write(bite);
            }
            System.out.println("Image copied successfully!");
        } catch (IOException e) {
            e.printStackTrace();
        }
    }
}
```

Expected Output: `Image copied successfully!`

Explanation: After running the ImageCopier program, there won't be any textual output to the console if everything goes correctly, except for the message indicating success. However, you should find a new file named `destination.jpg` in the same directory as your program, which is an exact copy of `source.jpg`. The console message would be as shown above.

To produce the expected output "Image copied successfully!" using the provided Java program, you need to ensure the following setup and input conditions are met:

1. Source File: There should be a file named `source.jpg` located in the directory from which the Java program is executed. This file must be accessible and readable.
2. Write Permission: The program must have the necessary permissions to write to the destination directory, as it attempts to create or overwrite the file named `destination.jpg` in the same directory.

If both conditions are satisfied (i.e., the `source.jpg` file exists and the program has permission to write in the directory), running the program will successfully copy the contents of `source.jpg` to `destination.jpg`, and it will print "Image copied successfully!" as output.

If either the source file is missing, unreadable, or the program lacks write permissions, the program will catch an `IOException` and print the stack trace instead of the success message.

Exercise 2: Character Stream Charm

Objective: Create a simple diary entry program that saves today's entry in a text file using character streams.

```
import java.io.FileWriter;
import java.io.IOException;
import java.util.Scanner;

public class DailyDiary {
    public static void main(String[] args) {
        try (FileWriter writer = new FileWriter("DiaryEntry.
txt", true);
             Scanner scanner = new Scanner(System.in)) {
            System.out.println("What's on your mind today?");
            String entry = scanner.nextLine();
            writer.write(entry + "\n");
            System.out.println("Your thoughts have been saved.
Reflect on them later.");
        } catch (IOException e) {
            e.printStackTrace();
        }
    }
}
```

```
Expected Output: What's on your mind today?
Your thoughts have been saved. Reflect on them later.
```

Explanation: The `DailyDiary` program will prompt the user for input and then save that input to a file named `DiaryEntry.txt`. Assuming the user types "Today was a good day." when prompted, the console output would be as shown above. And if you open `DiaryEntry.txt`, you would find a new line added with the text "Today was a good day."

Please note, for the `DailyDiary` program, the text "Today was a good day." is just an example. The actual output in the text file will depend on what the user types when prompted.

10.2 File Handling

Java's `File` class provides an abstract representation of file and directory pathnames, offering a wide array of methods to manipulate files and directories. This is crucial for applications that require direct interaction with the file system, such as creating log files, reading configuration files, or managing user data.

Exercise Creating Files

To create a new file, you'll use the createNewFile method of the File class. This method returns a boolean value: `true` if the file didn't exist and was successfully created, or `false` if the file already exists.

Example Program `FileCreator`:

```
import java.io.File;
import java.io.IOException;

public class FileCreator {
    public static void main(String[] args) {
        try {
            File myFile = new File("newFile.txt");
            if (myFile.createNewFile()) {
                System.out.println("File created: " + myFile.
getName());
            } else {
                System.out.println("File already exists.");
            }
```

```
    } catch (IOException e) {
            System.out.println("An error occurred.");
            e.printStackTrace();
        }
    }
}
```

Expected Outputs:

1. If the file `newFile.txt` does not exist in the directory where the program is run, the expected output is: `File created: newFile.txt`
2. If the file newFile.txt already exists, the expected output is: `File already exists.`

Exercise Deleting Files

To delete a file, you'll use the `delete` method, which also returns a boolean value indicating the success of the operation.

Example Program `FileDeleter`:

```
import java.io.File;

public class FileDeleter {
    public static void main(String[] args) {
        File myFile = new File("newFile.txt");
        if (myFile.delete()) {
            System.out.println("Deleted the file: " + myFile.
getName());
        } else {
            System.out.println("Failed to delete the file.");
        }
    }
}
```

Expected Outputs

If the file newFile.txt exists and is successfully deleted, the expected output is:

`Deleted the file: newFile.txt`

If the file does not exist or cannot be deleted (due to permission issues or the file being open in another application), the expected output is: `Failed to delete the file.`

Checking for File Existence

The exists method checks whether a file or directory exists at the path specified by the File object.

Example Program FileChecker:

```
import java.io.File;

public class FileChecker {
    public static void main(String[] args) {
        File myFile = new File("newFile.txt");
        if (myFile.exists()) {
            System.out.println("File exists: " + myFile.
getName());
        } else {
            System.out.println("File does not exist.");
        }
    }
}
```

Expected Outputs

1. If the file `newFile.txt` exists, the expected output is: `File exists: newFile.txt`
2. If the file does not exist, the expected output is: `File does not exist.`

Reading and Writing to Files

- Byte Streams: Use `FileInputStream` and `FileOutputStream` for handling raw binary data.
- Character Streams: Use `FileReader` and `FileWriter` for handling text data, which allows for character encoding (like UTF-8).

Fun Exercise `FileCopier`

Create a program named `FileCopier.java` that copies the content of one file to another using `FileInputStream` and `FileOutputStream`.

```
import java.io.FileInputStream;
import java.io.FileOutputStream;
import java.io.IOException;

public class FileCopier {
    public static void main(String[] args) {
        try (FileInputStream fis = new FileInputStream("source.
txt");
             FileOutputStream fos = new
FileOutputStream("destination.txt")) {

            int byteContent;
            while ((byteContent = fis.read()) != -1) {
                fos.write(byteContent);
            }
            System.out.println("Copy successful!");
        } catch (IOException e) {
            System.out.println("An error occurred during
copy.");
            e.printStackTrace();
        }
    }
}
```

Expected Outputs

1. Upon successful completion of copying the contents from `source.txt` to `destination.txt`, the expected output is:

```
Copy successful!
```

2. If there is an error during the copy operation, such as `source.txt` not existing or a problem with writing to `destination.txt`, the output will begin with:

```
An error occurred during copy.
```

And followed by the stack trace of the exception that occurred, which details the nature of the error.

After running `FileCopier.java`, check the contents of `destination.txt` to verify the copy operation. This practical example demonstrates file handling in a tangible and interactive manner, reinforcing the concepts of file I/O in Java.

10.3 Buffering Techniques

Buffering in Java I/O operations is a technique used to enhance the efficiency and performance of input and output processes. Instead of reading or writing one byte or character at a time, buffering allows a program to read or write a larger block of data in one go. This significantly reduces the number of I/O operations, making the process faster and more efficient, especially when dealing with large files or streams.

Benefits of Buffering:

- Increased Performance: By reducing the number of I/O operations, buffering can significantly speed up reading from and writing to files or other I/O sources.
- Efficient Data Handling: Buffering allows for the temporary storage of data during I/O operations, enabling more complex data processing tasks.
- Reduced Resource Usage: Fewer I/O operations mean less strain on system resources, improving the overall performance of the application.

Using `BufferedReader` and `BufferedWriter`:

Java provides `BufferedReader` and `BufferedWriter` classes in the `java.io` package to implement buffered I/O operations for character streams.

BufferedReader is used to read text from a character-input stream, buffering characters to provide efficient reading of characters, arrays, and lines.

BufferedWriter writes text to a character-output stream, buffering characters to provide efficient writing.

Example Program: Reading and Writing Files with Buffering

Let's create a fun and practical exercise by writing two simple programs: one that reads a poem from a file using `BufferedReader`, and another that writes a short story to a file using `BufferedWriter`.

Reading a Poem with `BufferedReader`:

```
import java.io.*;

public class PoemReader {
    public static void main(String[] args) {
        try (BufferedReader reader = new BufferedReader(new
FileReader("poem.txt"))) {
            String line;
            System.out.println("Reading poem from file:");
            while ((line = reader.readLine()) != null) {
                System.out.println(line);
            }
        } catch (IOException e) {
            System.out.println("An error occurred while reading
the poem.");
            e.printStackTrace();
        }
    }
}
```

Writing a Short Story with `BufferedWriter`:

```
import java.io.*;

public class StoryWriter {
    public static void main(String[] args) {
        String story = "Once upon a time, in a land far, far
away, there lived a brave little programmer.";

        try (BufferedWriter writer = new BufferedWriter(new
FileWriter("story.txt"))) {
            writer.write(story);
            System.out.println("Short story written to file
successfully!");
        } catch (IOException e) {
            System.out.println("An error occurred while writing
the story.");
            e.printStackTrace();
        }
    }
}
```

Fun Exercise:

The following exercises will not only help you practice buffered I/O operations but also encourage creativity and exploration of Java's powerful I/O capabilities. These exercises encourage interaction with the user and further exploration of file I/O in Java, making learning both fun and practical.

1. Modify the Poem: Change the PoemReader program to display the poem in reverse order, line by line.

Example Program `PoemReaderReverse`

```
import java.io.*;
import java.util.ArrayList;
import java.util.Collections;

public class PoemReaderReverse {
    public static void main(String[] args) {
        ArrayList<String> lines = new ArrayList<>();

        try (BufferedReader reader = new BufferedReader(new
FileReader("poem.txt"))) {
            String line;
            while ((line = reader.readLine()) != null) {
                lines.add(line);
            }
            Collections.reverse(lines); // Reverse the order of
lines
            System.out.println("Poem in reverse order:");
            for (String reversedLine : lines) {
                System.out.println(reversedLine);
            }
        } catch (IOException e) {
            System.out.println("An error occurred while reading
the poem.");
            e.printStackTrace();
        }
    }
}
```

Expected Output

Assuming `poem.txt` contains:
`Roses are red,`
`Violets are blue,`
`Sugar is sweet,`
`And so are you.`
	The expected output would be:
	`Poem in reverse order:`
	`And so are you.`
	`Sugar is sweet,`
	`Violets are blue,`
	`Roses are red,`

2. Add More to the Story: Extend the `StoryWriter` program to prompt the user for additional sentences to add to the story, appending each new sentence to `story.txt`.

Example Program `StoryWriterExtended`

```
import java.io.*;
import java.util.Scanner;

public class StoryWriterExtended {
    public static void main(String[] args) {
        Scanner scanner = new Scanner(System.in);
        System.out.println("Enter additional sentences to add
to the story (Type 'end' to finish):");

        try (BufferedWriter writer = new BufferedWriter(new
FileWriter("story.txt", true))) { // Append mode
            String inputLine;
            while (!(inputLine = scanner.nextLine()).
equalsIgnoreCase("end")) {
                writer.newLine(); // Move to a new line
                writer.write(inputLine);
                writer.flush(); // Flush to ensure each sentence
is written
            }
            System.out.println("Story updated successfully!");
        } catch (IOException e) {
            System.out.println("An error occurred while
updating the story.");
            e.printStackTrace();
        } finally {
            scanner.close();
        }
    }
}
```

Expected Output	

Sample Input
`The programmer wielded their keyboard like a sword.`
`They faced bugs and errors without fear.`
end
Assuming `story.txt` initially contains;
`Once upon a time, in a land far, far away, there lived a brave little programmer.`
	The expected output would be:
	`Enter additional sentences to add to the story (Type 'end' to finish):`
	`Story updated successfully!`
	After running the program and inputting the sample sentences, `story.txt` will be updated to:
	`Once upon a time, in a land far, far away, there lived a brave little programmer.`
	`The programmer wielded their keyboard like a sword.`
	`They faced bugs and errors without fear.`

10.4 Working with User Input

Understanding User Input with the Scanner Class

Java provides a very convenient way to handle user inputs through its `Scanner` class. This class can parse primitive types and strings using regular expressions. It can break down the input into tokens using a delimiter, which is by default whitespace. The `Scanner` class is part of the `java.util` package, so you need to import it at the beginning of your code.

Using the Scanner Class

To use the Scanner class for reading user input, you first need to create an instance of Scanner attached to the input source, which is usually `System.in` for console input.

Example Program

```
import java.util.Scanner;

public class InputExample {
    public static void main(String[] args) {
        Scanner scanner = new Scanner(System.in); // Create a
Scanner object

        System.out.println("Enter your name: ");
        String name = scanner.nextLine(); // Read user input

        System.out.println("Enter your age: ");
        int age = scanner.nextInt(); // Read integer input

        scanner.nextLine(); // Consume the leftover newline

        System.out.println("Enter your favorite quote: ");
        String quote = scanner.nextLine(); // Read a line of
input

        System.out.println("Your name is: " + name);
        System.out.println("Your age is: " + age);
        System.out.println("Your favorite quote is: \"" + quote
+ "\"");

        scanner.close(); // Close the scanner
    }
}
```

Expected Output

Depending on user input, the output will vary. Here's an example:

```
Enter your name:
John Doe
Enter your age:
30
Enter your favorite quote:
To be or not to be.
Your name is: John Doe
Your age is: 30
Your favorite quote is: "To be or not to be."
```

Fun and Practical Exercises

Exercise: Interactive Quiz

Create a simple interactive quiz that asks the user a couple of questions and then provides a score at the end.

Example Program `QuizProgram.java`

```
import java.util.Scanner;

public class QuizProgram {
    public static void main(String[] args) {
        Scanner scanner = new Scanner(System.in);
        int score = 0;

        System.out.println("Quiz Time!");
        System.out.println("Question 1: What is the capital of
France?");
        String answer1 = scanner.nextLine();
        if (answer1.equalsIgnoreCase("Paris")) {
            score++;
        }

        System.out.println("Question 2: How many continents are
there?");
        int answer2 = scanner.nextInt();
        if (answer2 == 7) {
            score++;
        }

        System.out.println("Your score is: " + score + "/2");
        scanner.close();
    }
}
```

Expected Output

Depending on the user's answers, the score will be displayed at the end.

For correct answers:

```
Quiz Time!
Question 1: What is the capital of France?
Paris
Question 2: How many continents are there?
7
Your score is: 2/2
```

These exercises, examples, and the practical use of the Scanner class should help beginners understand how to effectively handle user input in Java, making their programs interactive and responsive to user actions.

10.5 Serialization and Deserialization

Serialization is the process of converting an object into a stream of bytes to store the object or transmit it to memory, a database, or a file. Its main purpose is to save the state of an object in order to be able to recreate it when needed. The reverse process is called deserialization.

How Serialization Works in Java

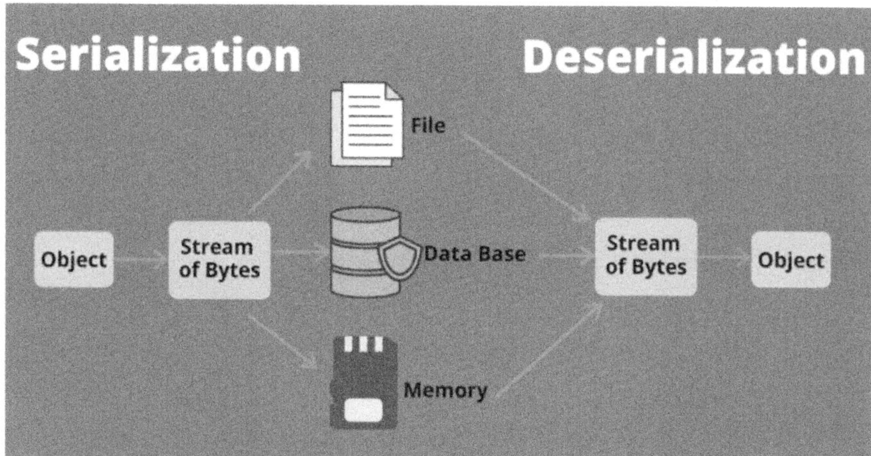

https://www.studytonight.com/java-examples/java-serialization-and-deserialization

Java provides a mechanism where you can serialize and deserialize objects using `ObjectOutputStream` and `ObjectInputStream` classes. To make a Java object serializable you implement the `java.io.Serializable` interface. This interface is a marker interface, meaning it does not contain any methods. It simply allows the serialization mechanism to verify that the class is able to be serialized.

Example: Serializing and Deserializing an Object

Let's consider a simple example where we have a `Student` class that implements the Serializable interface.

Example Program `Student.java`

```
import java.io.Serializable;

public class Student implements Serializable {
    private static final long serialVersionUID = 1L;
    private String name;
    private int age;

    public Student(String name, int age) {
        this.name = name;
        this.age = age;
    }

    @Override
    public String toString() {
        return "Student{name='" + name + "', age=" + age + '}';
    }
}
```

Serialization Example

```
import java.io.FileOutputStream;
import java.io.ObjectOutputStream;

public class SerializeExample {
    public static void main(String[] args) {
        Student student = new Student("John Doe", 22);
        try {
            FileOutputStream fileOut = new
FileOutputStream("student.ser");
            ObjectOutputStream out = new
ObjectOutputStream(fileOut);
            out.writeObject(student);
            out.close();
            fileOut.close();
            System.out.println("Serialized data is saved in
student.ser");
        } catch (Exception i) {
            i.printStackTrace();
        }
    }
}
```

Expected Output

```
Serialized data is saved in student.ser
```

Deserialization Example

```
import java.io.FileInputStream;
import java.io.ObjectInputStream;

public class DeserializeExample {
    public static void main(String[] args) {
        Student student = null;
        try {
            FileInputStream fileIn = new
FileInputStream("student.ser");
            ObjectInputStream in = new
ObjectInputStream(fileIn);
            student = (Student) in.readObject();
            in.close();
            fileIn.close();
        } catch (Exception i) {
            i.printStackTrace();
            return;
        }
        System.out.println("Deserialized Student...");
        System.out.println(student);
    }
}
```

Expected Output

```
Deserialized Student...
Student{name='John Doe', age=22}
```

Fun and Practical Exercise: Personal Diary

Create a simple diary application where users can save daily entries and retrieve them.

Example Program DiaryEntry.java

```
import java.io.Serializable;
import java.time.LocalDate;

public class DiaryEntry implements
Serializable {
   private LocalDate date;
     private String content;

     public DiaryEntry(LocalDate date,
String content) {
          this.date = date;
          this.content = content;
     }

     @Override
     public String toString() {
          return "DiaryEntry{" +
                  "date=" + date +
                  ", content='" + content
+ '\'' +
                  '}';
     }
}
```

Explanation
Imports
`java.io.Serializable`: This import statement is necessary because the DiaryEntry class implements the Serializable interface, which enables its instances to be serialized into a byte stream for file storage or transmission.
`java.time.LocalDate`: This is used for handling dates in a modern and efficient way. It represents a date without time-of-day information, which is suitable for diary entries that are typically associated with specific dates.
Class Declaration (public class DiaryEntry)
The class is declared as `public`, meaning it can be accessed from other classes.
It implements the `Serializable` interface, indicating objects of this class can be serialized.
Class Fields (public DiaryEntry)
`date`: A `LocalDate` object that stores the date associated with the diary entry. It's marked as `private` to encapsulate the data and restrict direct access from outside the class.
`content`: A `String` that holds the text content of the diary entry. This could be any personal note, observation, or description for the day.
Constructor
The constructor initializes new `DiaryEntry` objects with specific dates and content. It takes two parameters (`LocalDate date` and `String content`) and assigns them to the corresponding class fields.
toString Method @Override
This method overrides the `toString` method inherited from the `Object` class. It provides a string representation of a `DiaryEntry` object, which includes the date and content of the entry. This is particularly useful for displaying diary entries in a readable format when they are loaded from the file.

Explanation
The `DiaryEntry.java` program defines a data structure for storing individual diary entries, each associated with a specific date and containing some text content. By implementing the `Serializable` interface, instances of `DiaryEntry` can be easily saved to and retrieved from persistent storage, making it an essential part of creating a diary application that retains entries between runs. This program demonstrates fundamental concepts like class creation, data encapsulation, object serialization, and the use of Java's date and time API.

Serialization and Deserialization

You can extend the serialization and deserialization examples to include saving and loading diary entries. Create methods for adding new entries and retrieving them based on the date.

This exercise will help beginners understand how objects can be persisted and retrieved, making their Java applications capable of handling more complex data in a more user-friendly manner.

As an example, let's create a sample program for the diary management system. This program allows adding new diary entries and retrieving them based on the date. It uses serialization to save and load diary entries to and from a file as following:

Program `DiaryEntry.java`

```
import java.io.Serializable;
import java.util.Date;

public class DiaryEntry implements Serializable {
    private Date date;
    private String content;

    public DiaryEntry(Date date, String content) {
        this.date = date;
        this.content = content;
    }

    public Date getDate() {
        return date;
    }

    public String getContent() {
        return content;
    }

    @Override
    public String toString() {
        return "DiaryEntry{" +
                "date=" + date +
                ", content='" + content + '\'' +
                '}';
    }
}
```

Program `DiaryManager.java`

This class handles adding and retrieving diary entries using serialization and deserialization.

```
import java.io.*;
import java.util.*;

public class DiaryManager {
    private final String filePath = "diaryEntries.ser";
    private List<DiaryEntry> entries;

    public DiaryManager() {
        loadEntries();
    }

    private void loadEntries() {
        try (ObjectInputStream ois = new ObjectInputStream(new
FileInputStream(filePath))) {
            entries = (List<DiaryEntry>) ois.readObject();
        } catch (FileNotFoundException e) {
            entries = new ArrayList<>();
        } catch (IOException | ClassNotFoundException e) {
            e.printStackTrace();
        }
    }

    public void addEntry(DiaryEntry entry) {
        entries.add(entry);
        saveEntries();
    }

    private void saveEntries() {
        try (ObjectOutputStream oos = new ObjectOutputStream(new
FileOutputStream(filePath))) {
  oos.writeObject(entries);
        } catch (IOException e) {
            e.printStackTrace();
        }
    }
```

```
    public DiaryEntry getEntryByDate(Date date) {
        for (DiaryEntry entry : entries) {
            if (entry.getDate().equals(date)) {
                return entry;
            }
        }
        return null;
    }

    public static void main(String[] args) {
        DiaryManager manager = new DiaryManager();
        manager.addEntry(new DiaryEntry(new Date(), "Today was
a good day."));
        DiaryEntry entry = manager.getEntryByDate(new Date());
        System.out.println(entry);
    }
}
```

Sample Input	Sample Output

Let's say you run the `DiaryManager` class's `main` method on September 1, 2024, with the intention to add a diary entry for that day:
`Date: September 1, 2024`
`Content: "Today was a good day."`
	`DiaryEntry{date=Mon Sep 01 00:00:00 IST 2024, content='Today was a good day.'}`

Sample Output

After executing the `main` method, the program adds the new entry for September 1, 2024, and then retrieves and prints this entry. The expected output on the console would be as shown above.

The exact format of the date might vary depending on your system's locale and timezone settings. The key point is that the program successfully adds an entry, persists it, and then retrieves it based on the date, showcasing the principles of serialization and deserialization for beginners in a practical and fun exercise.

Explanation

- DiaryEntry.java: Defines a serializable diary entry with a date and content.
- DiaryManager.java: Manages diary entries. It loads existing entries from a file at initialization, adds new entries, saves entries to the file, and retrieves entries by date.
- main method: Demonstrates adding a new entry and then retrieving an entry based on today's date.

Expected Output

When running this program, it will add a new diary entry and then retrieve it based on today's date, printing the entry to the console. The exact output will depend on the current date and the content added.

10.6 Advanced Java I/O Operations for Beginners

`RandomAccessFile`: Exploring Non-Sequential File Access

Imagine you're reading a book and want to jump back and forth between chapters without having to flip through every page in between. In the world of computer files, `RandomAccessFile` makes this possible. It's a special tool in Java that lets you read from or write to any part of a file directly, without having to go through it sequentially from the start. This can be particularly useful when you're dealing with large files and you need to update or read a specific part quickly.

Example: Think of a music playlist file where each song is listed with details of title, artist, and length. If you wanted to update the length of the fifth song in the list, `RandomAccessFile` would let you go straight to the part of the file where that song's length is stored and update it, without having to read through the first four songs' details.

Example Program for `RandomAccessFile`

This simple example demonstrates how to use `RandomAccessFile` to write to a specific position in a file and then read from that position. We'll create a file named "`example.txt`" and insert a message at a specified position.

```
import java.io.RandomAccessFile;

public class RandomAccessFileExample {
    public static void main(String[] args) {
        try {
            // Creating a new RandomAccessFile
            RandomAccessFile file = new
RandomAccessFile("example.txt", "rw");

            // Moving the file pointer to position 200
            file.seek(200);

            // Writing a string at position 200
            file.writeUTF("This is a test message.");

            // Going back to the same position to read the
written message
            file.seek(200);

            // Reading the string from the file
            String result = file.readUTF();
            System.out.println("Read from file: " + result);

            // Closing the file
            file.close();
        } catch (Exception e) {
            e.printStackTrace();
        }
    }
}
```

Expected Output

```
Read from file: This is a test message.
```

NIO (New I/O): Enhancing Java's I/O Capabilities

As your Java journey progresses, you'll discover that some applications need to handle lots of data coming in and out simultaneously, akin to a bustling chat application that manages messages from thousands of users at once. Java's NIO (New Input/Output) is tailored for such scenarios, offering a more efficient way to handle I/O operations, which stands for Input/Output. It's an integral part of Java's toolkit for building scalable applications that can manage multiple data channels elegantly.

Why It's Important: NIO can help your applications perform better by utilizing system resources more wisely. It's comparable to having a highly efficient post office that can manage sending and receiving thousands of packages simultaneously without getting overwhelmed.

Where It Might Be Used: Imagine a game server where players from all around the world connect, interact, and update game states in real-time. NIO makes it possible to manage all these connections smoothly, ensuring that every player's experience is fast and responsive.

Example Program for NIO

This example demonstrates a basic use of Java NIO to read content from a file using a `ByteBuffer` and `Channels`. We'll read the contents of "example.txt" created in the previous example.

```
import java.nio.*;
import java.nio.channels.*;
import java.io.*;

public class SimpleNIOExample {
    public static void main(String[] args) {
        try {
            // Opening a file and getting a channel
            FileInputStream fis = new FileInputStream("example.
txt");
            FileChannel channel = fis.getChannel();

            // Creating a buffer to read data
            ByteBuffer buffer = ByteBuffer.allocate(1024);

            // Reading data from the channel into the buffer
            channel.read(buffer);

             // Flipping the buffer from writing mode to
reading mode
             buffer.flip();
            // Converting bytes to string
            String fileContent = new String(buffer.array(),
buffer.position(), buffer.limit());
            System.out.println("File content: " + fileContent.
trim());
```

```
        // Closing the channel and the stream
            channel.close();
            fis.close();
        } catch (IOException e) {
            e.printStackTrace();
        }
    }
}
```

Expected Output

```
File content: (content of example.txt up to 1024 characters)
```

Note: The output will depend on the content of "example.txt", especially the part written by the `RandomAccessFileExample`.

These examples illustrate the basics of using `RandomAccessFile` and NIO in Java. For more advanced use cases, such as non-sequential file access with `RandomAccessFile` or scalable I/O operations with NIO, further exploration and practice are encouraged.

Encouragement for Further Exploration

While RandomAccessFile and NIO are more advanced topics, understanding what they are and why they're useful gives you a glimpse into the powerful capabilities Java offers for building robust and high-performing applications. As you grow more comfortable with Java's basics, revisiting these concepts can open new doors to exciting programming challenges and opportunities.

Remember, every expert was once a beginner, and every complex concept can be understood with time, curiosity, and practice. So, consider these advanced topics as landmarks on your Java learning journey, signaling exciting territories to explore as you advance further.

10.7 Practical Exercises

Exercise 1: Word Counter

Objective: Create a program that reads a text file and counts the occurrence of each word. Write the results to a new file, where each line contains a word followed by its count.

Steps:

1. Read the contents of a file named "`input.txt`".
2. Split the text into words and count the occurrence of each.
3. Write the results to a file named "`wordCount.txt`", with each word and its count on a new line.

Sample Program

```
import java.io.*;
import java.util.*;

public class WordCount {
    public static void main(String[] args) {
        // File paths
        String inputFilePath = "input.txt";
        String outputFilePath = "wordCount.txt";

        // Use a HashMap to store each word and its count
        Map<String, Integer> wordCounts = new HashMap<>();

        try {
            // Open the file for reading
            File inputFile = new File(inputFilePath);
            Scanner scanner = new Scanner(inputFile);

            // Read the file word by word
            while (scanner.hasNext()) {
                String word = scanner.next().toLowerCase(); //
Convert word to lower case for uniformity
                wordCounts.put(word, wordCounts.getOrDefault(word,
0) + 1); // Update count
            }
            scanner.close(); // Close the scanner

            // Open the file for writing
            PrintWriter writer = new
PrintWriter(outputFilePath);

            // Write each word and its count to the file
            for (Map.Entry<String, Integer> entry : wordCounts.
entrySet()) {
```

```
            writer.println(entry.getKey() + " " + entry.
getValue());
            }
            writer.close(); // Close the writer

            System.out.println("Word count has been written to
" + outputFilePath);

        } catch (FileNotFoundException e) {
            System.err.println("File not found: " +
e.getMessage());
        }
    }
}
```

Sample Input (input.txt)	Expected Output (wordCount.txt):

`Hello world`
`Hello Java`
`Java world`
	`Hello: 2`
	`world: 2`
	`Java: 2`

Exercise 2: Data Filter

Objective: Write a program that reads a CSV file containing multiple columns of data. Filter the rows based on a specific condition (e.g., all values greater than a certain number in a certain column) and write the filtered rows to a new CSV file.

Steps:

1. Read data from "data.csv".
2. Filter rows where the second column's value is greater than 50.
3. Write the filtered rows to "filteredData.csv".

Sample Program

```
import java.io.BufferedReader;
import java.io.BufferedWriter;
import java.io.FileReader;
import java.io.FileWriter;
import java.io.IOException;

public class CSVFilter {
    public static void main(String[] args) {
```

```
        // Input and Output file paths
        String inputFilePath = "path/to/input.csv";
        String outputFilePath = "path/to/output.csv";

        // Open the input CSV file for reading
        try (BufferedReader br = new BufferedReader(new
FileReader(inputFilePath));
             BufferedWriter bw = new BufferedWriter(new
FileWriter(outputFilePath))) {

            String line;
            // Read the header and write it to the output file
directly
            if ((line = br.readLine()) != null) {
                bw.write(line);
                bw.newLine();
            }

            // Read each subsequent line from the input CSV
            while ((line = br.readLine()) != null) {
                String[] values = line.split(","); // Assuming
a comma delimiter

                // Check if the second column's value is
greater than 50
                // Note: Assuming the second column contains
numeric values
                if (Integer.parseInt(values[1].trim()) > 50) {
                    // Write the filtered line to the output CSV
file
                    bw.write(line);
                    bw.newLine();
                }
            }
        } catch (IOException e) {
            e.printStackTrace();
        }
    }
}
```

Sample Input (data.csv)	Expected Output (filteredData.csv):

`Name,Score`
`John,45`
`Doe,75`
`Jane,60`
	`Name,Score`
	`Doe,75`
	`Jane,60`

Explanation:

This program assumes that the CSV file uses a comma (,) as the delimiter and that the second column contains integer values. You'll need to modify the inputFilePath and outputFilePath variables to point to the actual paths of your input and output CSV files.

The program first reads and writes the header (if present) to ensure the output CSV maintains the same structure as the input. It then processes each line, splitting it into an array of String values based on the comma delimiter. It checks the value of the second column (index 1 in the array) to see if it's greater than 50. If the condition is met, the program writes the entire row to the output CSV file.

Exercise 3: Interactive Quiz

Objective: Create a console-based quiz application that asks the user multiple-choice questions, takes their input for answers, calculates the score, and displays the result.

Steps:

1. Display a question and a list of multiple-choice answers.
2. Prompt the user to select an answer.
3. Repeat for multiple questions.
4. At the end, display the user's score.

Sample Program

```
import java.util.Scanner;

public class QuizApplication {
    public static void main(String[] args) {
        // Questions
        String[] questions = {
            "What is the capital of France?",
            "Who is the CEO of Tesla?",
            "What is 2 + 2?",
            "What language is this program written in?"
        };

        // Choices
        String[][] choices = {
            {"1. Paris", "2. London", "3. Berlin", "4.
Madrid"},
            {"1. Bill Gates", "2. Steve Jobs", "3. Elon Musk",
"4. Jeff Bezos"},
            {"1. 3", "2. 4", "3. 5", "4. 6"},
            {"1. Python", "2. Java", "3. C#", "4. JavaScript"}
        };

        // Correct Answers (index corresponds to the correct
choice)
        int[] answers = {1, 3, 2, 2};

        int score = 0;
        Scanner scanner = new Scanner(System.in);

        // Iterate through each question
        for (int i = 0; i < questions.length; i++) {
            System.out.println(questions[i]);

            // Display choices for each question
            for (String choice : choices[i]) {
                System.out.println(choice);
            }

            System.out.print("Enter your choice (1-4): ");
            int userAnswer = scanner.nextInt();
```

```
            // Check if the answer is correct
            if (userAnswer == answers[i]) {
                score++;
                System.out.println("Correct!");
            } else {
                System.out.println("Wrong!");
            }

            System.out.println(); // Newline for formatting
        }

        // Display the final score
        System.out.println("You scored " + score + " out of " +
questions.length);

        scanner.close();
    }
}
```

Example Interaction:

```
What is the capital of France?
1. Paris
2. London
3. Berlin
4. Madrid
Enter your choice (1-4): 1
Correct!

Who is the CEO of Tesla?
1. Bill Gates
2. Steve Jobs
3. Elon Musk
4. Jeff Bezos
Enter your choice (1-4): 3
Correct!

What is 2 + 2?
1. 3
2. 4
3. 5
4. 6
Enter your choice (1-4): 2
Correct!
```

```
What language is this program written in?
1. Python
2. Java
3. C#
4. JavaScript
Enter your choice (1-4): 2
Correct!

You scored 4 out of 4
```

This interaction demonstrates the program flow from presenting questions and choices, collecting user responses, and finally displaying the total score. The user correctly answered all questions in this example, achieving a perfect score.

Fun Challenge: Personal Diary

Objective: Develop a console-based application that allows users to maintain a personal diary. Users can add new diary entries with dates and read entries by entering a specific date.

Features:

1. Add a new diary entry with the current date.
2. Read an entry by entering a date.
3. Save entries to a file and load them when the program starts.

Sample Program

```
import java.io.*;
import java.time.LocalDate;
import java.util.HashMap;
import java.util.Scanner;

public class PersonalDiary {
    private static final String FILE_PATH = "diaryEntries.dat";
    private HashMap<LocalDate, DiaryEntry> entries = new
HashMap<>();

    public PersonalDiary() {
        loadEntries();
    }
```

```
    public void addEntry(LocalDate date, String content) {
        DiaryEntry entry = new DiaryEntry(date, content);
        entries.put(date, entry);
        saveEntries();
        System.out.println("Diary entry added successfully.");
    }

    public void readEntry(LocalDate date) {
        DiaryEntry entry = entries.get(date);
        if (entry != null) {
            System.out.println("Entry for " + date + ": " +
entry.getContent());
        } else {
            System.out.println("No entry found for this
date.");
        }
    }

    @SuppressWarnings("unchecked")
    private void loadEntries() {
        try (ObjectInputStream ois = new ObjectInputStream(new
FileInputStream(FILE_PATH))) {
            entries = (HashMap<LocalDate, DiaryEntry>) ois.
readObject();
        } catch (FileNotFoundException e) {
            System.out.println("Diary file not found. A new
diary will be started.");
        } catch (IOException | ClassNotFoundException e) {
            e.printStackTrace();
        }
    }

    private void saveEntries() {
        try (ObjectOutputStream oos = new
ObjectOutputStream(new FileOutputStream(FILE_PATH))) {
            oos.writeObject(entries);
        } catch (IOException e) {
            e.printStackTrace();
        }
    }
```

```
    public static void main(String[] args) {
        Scanner scanner = new Scanner(System.in);
        PersonalDiary diary = new PersonalDiary();

        while (true) {
            System.out.println("Personal Diary Application");
            System.out.println("1. Add New Entry");
            System.out.println("2. Read Entry By Date");
            System.out.println("3. Exit");
            System.out.print("Choose an option: ");
            int option = scanner.nextInt();
            scanner.nextLine(); // consume newline

            switch (option) {
                case 1:
                    System.out.print("Enter your diary entry:
");
                    String content = scanner.nextLine();
                    diary.addEntry(LocalDate.now(), content);
                    break;
                case 2:
                    System.out.print("Enter date (YYYY-MM-DD):
");
                    LocalDate date = LocalDate.parse(scanner.
nextLine());
                    diary.readEntry(date);
                    break;
                case 3:
                    System.out.println("Exiting
application...");
                    return;
                default:
                    System.out.println("Invalid option. Please
try again.");
            }
        }
    }
}
```

Example Interaction:

```
Personal Diary Application
1. Add New Entry
2. Read Entry By Date
3. Exit
Choose an option: 1
Enter your diary entry: Today was a good day. I learned about
serialization in Java.
Diary entry added successfully.

Personal Diary Application
1. Add New Entry
2. Read Entry By Date
3. Exit
Choose an option: 2
Enter date (YYYY-MM-DD): 2024-01-28
Entry for 2024-01-28: Today was a good day. I learned about
serialization in Java.

Personal Diary Application
1. Add New Entry
2. Read Entry By Date
3. Exit
Choose an option: 1
Enter your diary entry: I started a new book on Java
programming.
Diary entry added successfully.

Personal Diary Application
1. Add New Entry
2. Read Entry By Date
3. Exit
Choose an option: 2
Enter date (YYYY-MM-DD): 2024-01-29
Entry for 2024-01-29: I started a new book on Java programming.

Personal Diary Application
1. Add New Entry
2. Read Entry By Date
3. Exit
Choose an option: 3
Exiting application...
```

This interaction demonstrates how a user can add new entries to their diary with the current date, read entries based on a specific date, and exit the application. Each time an entry is added, it's saved to the file, ensuring that data isn't lost between sessions. When the user chooses to read an entry by entering a specific date, the application retrieves and displays the content of the diary entry for that date if it exists.

This application lets users add new diary entries, read entries by date, and automatically saves the entries to a file named `diaryEntries.dat`. When the application starts, it attempts to load existing entries from this file.

10.8 Check Your Understanding

1. **What method would you use to check if a file exists in Java?**
   A) `File.existsFile()`
   B) `File.isFileExists()`
   C) `File.exists()`
   D) `File.checkExists()`
2. **Which of the following is true about serialization in Java?**
   A) It converts an object into a character stream.
   B) It is the process of writing data to a text file.
   C) It converts an object into a byte stream for storage or transmission.
   D) It only works with primitive data types.
3. **Which class is used for reading character files in Java?**
   A) `FileReader`
   B) `FileInputStream`
   C) `BufferedReader`
   D) `InputStreamReader`
4. **What is the primary advantage of using NIO over traditional I/O in Java?**
   A) NIO supports only file operations.
   B) NIO provides better performance for scalable applications.
   C) NIO can only operate in blocking mode.
   D) NIO does not support reading and writing operations.
5. **Which method is used to read a line of text from a file in Java?**
   A) `readLine()` from `BufferedReader`

B) `read()` from `FileReader`
C) `scanLine()` from `Scanner`
D) `getNextLine()` from `FileInputStream`

Answers:
1. C) `File.exists()`
2. C) It converts an object into a byte stream for storage or transmission.
3. A) `FileReader`
4. B) NIO provides better performance for scalable applications.
5. A) `readLine()` from `BufferedReader`

Programming Exercises

6. **(File Creation and Writing) Write a Java program that creates a new file named "Greetings.txt" and writes the following three lines into it:**

```
Hello, World!
Welcome to Java I/O.
Goodbye!
```

After writing to the file, read the file content and print it to the console.

7. **(User Input and Serialization) Create a simple Java application that does the following:**
   - Takes a user's name and age as input from the console.
   - Creates a `User` object with the name and age.
   - Serializes the `User` object to a file named "UserData.ser".
   - Deserializes the "UserData.ser" file back into a `User` object and prints the name and age to the console.

For these exercises, make sure to include error handling, especially for I/O operations, to practice good programming habits.

Sample Answers for Programming Exercises

6. File Creation and Writing

```
import java.io.BufferedWriter;
import java.io.File;
import java.io.FileWriter;
import java.io.IOException;

public class GreetingsFile {
    public static void main(String[] args) {
        // Define the file path
        String filePath = "Greetings.txt";
        File file = new File(filePath);
        // Try-with-resources to auto-close the writer
        try (BufferedWriter writer = new BufferedWriter(new
FileWriter(file))) {
            // Write lines to the file
            writer.write("Hello, World!\n");
            writer.write("Welcome to Java I/O.\n");
            writer.write("Goodbye!");
            System.out.println("File written successfully.");
        } catch (IOException e) {
            System.err.println("Error writing the file: " +
e.getMessage());
        }
    }
}
```

Expected Output:

```
File written successfully.
```

7. User Input and Serialization

```
import java.io.*;
import java.util.Scanner;

class User implements Serializable {
    private String name;
    private int age;

    public User(String name, int age) {
        this.name = name;
        this.age = age;
    }

    public String getName() {
        return name;
    }

    public int getAge() {
        return age;
    }
}
```

```
public class UserSerializationDemo {
    public static void main(String[] args) {
        Scanner scanner = new Scanner(System.in);
        System.out.print("Enter your name: ");
        String name = scanner.nextLine();

        System.out.print("Enter your age: ");
        int age = scanner.nextInt();

        User user = new User(name, age);
        String filename = "UserData.ser";

        // Serialize
        try (ObjectOutputStream out = new
ObjectOutputStream(new FileOutputStream(filename))) {
            out.writeObject(user);
            System.out.println("User data serialized.");
        } catch (IOException e) {
            System.err.println("Error serializing user data: "
+ e.getMessage());
        }

        // Deserialize
        try (ObjectInputStream in = new ObjectInputStream(new
FileInputStream(filename))) {
            User deserializedUser = (User) in.readObject();
            System.out.println("Deserialized User Object: ");
            System.out.println("Name: " + deserializedUser.
getName() + ", Age: " + deserializedUser.getAge());
        } catch (IOException | ClassNotFoundException e) {
            System.err.println("Error deserializing user data:
" + e.getMessage());
        }
    }
}
```

Expected Output:

```
Enter your name: John Doe
Enter your age: 30
User data serialized.
Deserialized User Object:
Name: John Doe, Age: 30
``` &#8203;``□oaicite:0□``&#8203;
```
```

Summary of Key Concepts

In Chapter 10, we dove into the essentials of Java Input and Output (I/O), a critical aspect of developing real-world Java applications. This chapter provided an introduction to the concept of streams and the File class, laying the groundwork for understanding how Java applications interact with external data sources. We explored different types of streams - byte and character streams - and discussed the hierarchy of I/O streams, emphasizing the significance of buffering techniques for enhancing I/O efficiency.

The chapter further detailed file handling techniques, demonstrating how to create, delete, and check the existence of files, alongside reading from and writing to files. Practical examples and exercises were provided to solidify these concepts, including the use of FileInputStream and FileOutputStream for byte streams, as well as FileReader and FileWriter for character streams.

Buffering techniques were introduced, highlighting the use of BufferedReader and BufferedWriter to improve I/O operations' efficiency. We then moved on to handling user input with the Scanner class, showing how to read various data types from the console.

Serialization and deserialization formed another crucial section where we discussed object persistence, enabling applications to save and retrieve complex data structures. Practical exercises demonstrated the serialization and deserialization processes using `ObjectOutputStream` and `ObjectInputStream`.

The chapter also ventured into advanced I/O operations, offering a gentle introduction to RandomAccessFile and the New I/O (NIO) package for scalable applications. These advanced topics were presented in a manner accessible to beginners, sparking interest in further exploration.

Finally, we wrapped up with practical exercises designed to apply the concepts learned. These exercises ranged from reading and processing data from files, managing user input, and implementing serialization and deserialization, providing a comprehensive hands-on experience.

Key Concepts

1. Streams: Understanding byte and character streams is essential for performing I/O operations in Java, allowing for efficient data read and write.

2. File Handling: Mastery of the File class and its methods is crucial for manipulating files, including creating, deleting, and checking files' existence.
3. Buffering Techniques: Buffering is vital for enhancing the efficiency of I/O operations, reducing the number of interactions with the underlying data source.
4. User Input Handling: The Scanner class is instrumental in building interactive Java applications, enabling the reading of various data types from the console.
5. Serialization and Deserialization: These processes are key to saving and retrieving application state, crucial for applications that manage complex data structures.
6. Advanced I/O Operations: An introduction to RandomAccessFile and NIO paves the way for building scalable applications that handle I/O operations more efficiently.

Importance of Mastering Java I/O

Mastering Java I/O is indispensable for developing robust Java applications that interact with external data sources, user input, and manage application state effectively. The skills acquired in this chapter lay the foundation for building complex, real-world applications, enabling developers to handle a wide range of I/O scenarios confidently. From simple file manipulations to managing serialized objects and implementing scalable I/O solutions, the knowledge of Java I/O is a cornerstone for modern application development.

Chapter 11: The Journey to Becoming a Software Engineer in Java

Embarking on a career in software engineering is a thrilling adventure filled with endless possibilities. For beginners aspiring to dive into the vibrant world of programming, Java stands out as a beacon, offering a robust platform to build versatile and scalable applications. This chapter aims to demystify the journey, providing a roadmap for novices to transition from beginners to professional Java developers.

11.1 Embracing the Basics of Java

The first step in your journey is to grasp the core concepts of Java. Begin with understanding variables, data types, control structures, and arrays. These fundamental building blocks form the foundation upon which your Java knowledge will grow.

Fun Exercise: Try creating a simple Java program that calculates the average of a set of numbers input by the user. This exercise will test your understanding of variables, arrays, loops, and user input in Java.

11.2 Diving Into Object-Oriented Programming (OOP)

Java is renowned for its object-oriented programming capabilities, emphasizing objects and classes. Familiarize yourself with key OOP concepts such as encapsulation, inheritance, polymorphism, and abstraction. These principles are not just academic; they are practical tools that will help you design and develop robust Java applications.

Practical Example: Design a basic "Car" class encapsulating properties like model, color, and horsepower. Then, extend this class to create specific car models. This will help you understand how inheritance and polymorphism work in Java.

11.3 Mastering Error Handling and Exceptions

A significant part of programming in Java - or any language - revolves around dealing with unexpected situations in your code. Learn about Java's exception handling mechanisms, including try-catch blocks, to write resilient and error-free applications.

Fun Exercise: Modify the "Car" class to throw a custom exception if an invalid horsepower value is set. This exercise will deepen your understanding of exceptions and how they can be used to enforce data integrity.

11.4 Leveraging Java's Rich API and Libraries

Java boasts a vast ecosystem of libraries and APIs, enabling developers to perform a wide range of tasks, from handling date and time operations to networking and file I/O. Start exploring Java's standard library, and practice using different classes and methods to solve common programming tasks.

Practical Exercise: Write a Java program that reads a file containing a list of Car models and their details, then filters and prints out cars with horsepower greater than 250. This will introduce you to file I/O operations in Java.

11.5 Exploring Frameworks and Tools

As you become more comfortable with Java's core features, begin exploring popular frameworks such as Spring and Hibernate. These frameworks can significantly speed up the development process for web and enterprise applications.

Challenge: Try building a simple CRUD (Create, Read, Update, Delete) application using Spring Boot. This will give you a taste of developing web applications with Java.

11.6 Collaborating and Version Control

Software development is often a team effort. Learn about version control systems like Git and platforms like GitHub to manage your code, collaborate with others, and contribute to open-source projects. These tools are essential for any aspiring software engineer.

Fun Exercise: Create a GitHub account, and start a new repository for your Java projects. Practice cloning the repository, making changes, and pushing updates. This will introduce you to the basics of version control and collaboration.

11.7 Continuous Learning and Networking

The field of software engineering is always evolving. Stay curious, continue learning new technologies and best practices, and connect with the community. Attend meetups, participate in coding challenges, and contribute to open-source projects to gain experience and build your network.

Actionable Tip: Join online forums and social media groups focused on Java programming. Engage with the community by asking questions, sharing your projects, and offering help to others.

Conclusion: Your Path to Becoming a Software Engineer

Your journey to becoming a software engineer is unique and filled with opportunities for growth and learning. By mastering Java, embracing its ecosystem, and engaging with the community, you're setting the stage for a rewarding career in software development. Remember, persistence, practice, and a passion for technology are your best allies on this journey. Welcome to the world of Java programming - your adventure begins now!

End-of-Book Review Page

Just One Click!

The world is about to open up for you – and that puts you in a great position to share this information with more people.

Simply by sharing your honest opinion of this book and a little about your own experience, you'll help others to find the accessible Java programming guidance they've been looking for.

https://www.amazon.com/review/review-your-purchases/?asin=B0DFV594TD

Thank you for your support. I wish you every success in your endeavors.

Bonus Chapter: Unlocking Your Programming Potential

In the digital age, coding isn't just a skill - it's your ticket to a world of opportunities, with entry-level programming roles offering salaries starting from $78,000. This chapter isn't just a guide; it's your roadmap to transforming your interest in programming into a thriving career. Here, we'll explore educational paths, internships, career opportunities, and, importantly, the ultimate resources to turbocharge your Java learning and beyond.

Discover ChatGPT: Your AI Companion in Coding

Imagine a digital companion, ChatGPT, that's designed to make coding, writing, and even email drafting as seamless as texting a friend. It's here to assist you 24/7, answering questions and guiding you through coding puzzles with ease.

Harnessing ChatGPT for Java Mastery

ChatGPT is a groundbreaking tool that transforms your ideas into executable code across languages like Java, Python, and more. It's your shortcut to developing applications, debugging code, and refining your programming skills - all while saving you time and boosting productivity.

The Magic of Prompt Engineering

Dive into the art of Prompt Engineering, where the right questions unlock AI's vast capabilities, making it a potent ally in your coding quests. It's about guiding ChatGPT to understand your coding dilemmas and provide tailored, intelligent solutions.

Accelerate Your Journey with ChatGPT

Utilize ChatGPT to accelerate your coding skills. Whether you're deciphering complex concepts, debugging, or translating code, ChatGPT is an indispensable resource that makes learning not just quicker but richer.

Launching Your Programming Career

Who says you need experience to break into the programming world? With dedication, creativity, and the right strategy, you can carve out your path in the tech landscape. We delve into practical steps to enhance your coding prowess, showcase your skills, and connect with the community-all pivotal moves towards securing that dream job.

1. **Improve your coding skills** – keep learning how to code in Java and practice regularly to improve your skills. Read more books with hands-on projects, such as "Learn Java in One Day and Learn It Well" to improve your coding skills.
2. **Create a portfolio** – you can create a website to host your portfolio or use a platform like LinkedIn to showcase your skills and previous projects to potential employers.
3. **Build your online presence** – create profiles online on platforms, such as LinkedIn, Twitter, Instagram, and other popular sites to build your online presence.
4. **Network with other programmers** – connect with other programmers locally and online in coding social communities to exchange ideas and learn from each other.
5. **Figure out the industry where you want to work** – as a programmer, you can work in any industry and sector out there. Based on your personal interests, pick a suitable industry where you want to work.
6. **Earn certifications** – continue to learn and earn certifications to boost your portfolio. Many online platforms, such as Udemy offer tests you can do to earn free or paid certifications.
7. **Take part in coding challenges or competitions** – search online for coding competitions or challenges to try. This is a good way to apply your coding skills while getting a chance to earn a prize (monetary).
8. **Join/start a club in your school** – if you're in a tech school learning programming or intend to join one, join an existing coding club or start one. You'll meet like-minded individuals with unique skills and potential in such clubs.
9. **Write a strong resume** – you'll present your resume to potential employers when making job applications. Work on your resume and ensure it reflects your skills and interests accurately. You can even hire professional resume-writing services to ensure you have a strong resume.
10. **Build projects** – develop programs as you practice and hone your skills to build projects for your portfolio to show potential employers.

11. **Contribute to open source projects** – the internet is home to many open source coding platforms, such as Git, that allow developers to collaborate on projects. Find a project you can join and contribute to improve your skills and better your portfolio.
12. **Find free programs you can join to help jumpstart your education or training** – look for internship opportunities in your city or online to kick-start your career in programming.

Your Gateway to Java Mastery: 28 Top Resources

Embark on an enriching journey to Java mastery with these curated resources. Each offers unique learning paths, practical exercises, and the support you need to progress from beginner to pro:

1. Codecademy: Dive into Java with free courses tailored for all levels.
2. Udemy: Explore a wide array of Java courses and tutorials.
3. Coursera: Benefit from high-quality tutorials and classes.
4. Java Code Geeks: Access Java tutorials, code samples, and eBooks.
5. Learn Java: Engage with interactive tutorials and a built-in code compiler.
6. Oracle Java Tutorials: Learn Java directly from the creators.
7. edX: Discover both free and paid Java courses.
8. Skillshare: Join online classes with peer reviews.
9. SoloLearn: Navigate comprehensive guides for beginners.
10. W3Resource: Utilize tutorials, code samples, and exercises.
11. Codementor: Find courses, tutorials, and coding tips.
12. Program Creek: Start with articles and tutorials for beginners.
13. Tutorials Point: Access quality content and practical exercises.
14. Java Beginners Tutorial: Explore fundamental topics and code examples.
15. Udacity: Enroll in basic online courses with a global student community.
16. Studytonight: Benefit from tutorials, codes, and exercises.
17. Treehouse: Enjoy video tutorials with a free trial.
18. Cave of Programming: Access free online courses with enrollment.
19. Sanfoundry: Practice with Java questions for all levels.
20. Programming by Doing: Challenge yourself with comprehensive courses and assignments.

21. JavaTpoint: Explore tutorials for learners at all levels.
22. Java Tutorial: Access courses from beginner to advanced.
23. Guru99: Discover free tutorials for beginners to pros.
24. JournalDev: Find Java courses arranged from basic to expert levels.
25. W3Schools: Learn with course content and samples.
26. Lynda.com (LinkedIn Learning): Find Java classes for all skill levels.
27. Programiz: Enjoy simple, high-quality tutorials.
28. Jenkov.com: Begin with tutorial courses for novices.

Beyond Java: Exploring New Languages

Your journey doesn't stop at Java. Explore HTML, CSS, SQL, JavaScript, Python, and C++ to broaden your development horizons and unlock new opportunities.

Embrace the Journey

Congratulations on taking the first step towards mastering Java and setting the foundation for a promising career in programming. Remember, practice is key - keep experimenting, building projects, and learning from your experiences.

If this book has guided you along your path, consider sharing your thoughts with a review or recommending it to friends embarking on their own coding journeys.

Here's to your success in programming and beyond - may your journey be filled with discovery, growth, and fulfillment. Happy coding!

Kudos on purchasing this book and embarking on your Java learning journey! If you've found value in it, consider leaving a positive review on Amazon to share your experience. Don't hesitate to let your friends know what you enjoyed about the book, too. Best wishes on your future projects and good luck as you embark on your path to becoming a software engineer!

Glossary

Assignment Operators: shortcuts in Java used to save time when you want to perform an operation on a variable and then save the result back into the same variable. For example, `x += 1;` is a quicker way to say "add 1 to `x` and then store the new value back into `x`." They help make your code cleaner and easier to read by combining an arithmetic operation (addition, subtraction, multiplication, or division) with assignment in one step.

API (Application Programming Interface): A set of rules and tools for building software applications, specifying how software components should interact.

Array: A way to store multiple items, such as numbers or text, in a single variable. Think of it as a shelf where each section holds a different item. In Java, an array organizes these items in a line, so you can easily find and manage them using their position, or index. This makes handling groups of related data simpler and more efficient.

Bitwise Operators: See Operators

Branching or Jump Statements: commands that change the usual line-by-line running order of code. They're like choosing different paths based on certain conditions or wanting to skip some steps. The most common ones are `break`, to exit loops; `continue`, to skip to the next loop iteration; and `return`, to exit methods. These statements help control the flow of your program, making it react differently under various conditions or scenarios.

Buffering: A technique used in programming to manage how data is stored or transferred. Imagine you're pouring a large jug of water into a series of smaller cups. Instead of pouring directly from the jug into each cup one by one, you use a funnel to control the flow and prevent spills. In computer terms, a buffer is similar to a funnel – it's a temporary holding area where data can be stored until it's ready to be used. This is especially helpful when data is being moved between different parts of a program or from a program to a device such as a hard drive or the internet. Buffering helps make these processes smoother and faster, reducing waiting times and ensuring data isn't lost or overwhelmed during transfer.

Bytecode: Intermediate code generated from compiling Java source code, which the Java Virtual Machine (JVM) can execute.

Class: A blueprint from which individual objects are created, containing methods and variables.

Collections: Advanced and flexible containers for storing groups of objects. Unlike arrays, which have a fixed size, collections can grow or shrink in size dynamically, making it easier to add or remove items as needed. They come in various forms, such as lists, sets, and maps, each offering different ways to organize and access data. Collections make managing groups of data more powerful and convenient, allowing for more complex data handling tasks.

Compiler: A tool that translates source code written in a high-level programming language (like Java) into machine code, bytecode, or another programming language.

Control Flow: The order in which individual statements, instructions, or function calls are executed or evaluated in a program. In Java, control flow mechanisms such as "if-else" statements, loops (for, while), and switch cases allow your program to make decisions, repeat tasks, and navigate different paths of execution based on certain conditions. This helps in creating dynamic and responsive programs that can adapt to different inputs or situations.

Data Type: A classification that specifies the type of data a variable can hold, such as numbers, text, or a combination of both. In Java, data types help the program understand how to use the data, for example, whether it's acceptable to add two values together or join texts. They ensure that operations on data are performed correctly and safely.

Debugging: The process of finding and fixing errors or "bugs" in a program. You may compare this process as being a detective or a teacher grading an essay, carefully examining your code to spot mistakes or issues that prevent the program from working correctly. In Java, debugging involves using tools and strategies to understand why a program isn't behaving as expected, making the necessary corrections to ensure it runs smoothly.

Deserialization: The reverse process of serialization. It's akin to taking the picture of the sculpture and using it to recreate the sculpture in another place. In Java, deserialization converts the byte stream back into a copy of the original object, restoring its state (data) so that a program can use it as if it were the original object itself.

Eclipse: An open-source integrated development environment (IDE) used for Java programming, among other languages.

Exceptions: Unexpected roadblocks that happen while a Java program is running, causing it to take a wrong turn or stop. They occur when something goes wrong, such as trying to open a file that doesn't exist or dividing a number by zero. Java uses exceptions to signal these problems so the program can either fix the issue or gracefully stop, preventing it from crashing.

File Handling: Creating, reading, writing, and manipulating files. Imagine keeping a diary where you jot down your thoughts (writing), read them later (reading), add new entries (creating), or erase something (manipulating). Java provides tools and classes that allow your programs to do these tasks with files on your computer, helping you manage data stored as documents, images, or any other file types.

Garbage Collection: Automatic memory management in Java, where the JVM automatically deletes objects that are no longer being used to free up resources.

GitHub: A cloud-based platform that facilitates version control and collaboration on software development projects. It harnesses the power of Git, a distributed version control system, allowing multiple developers to work on a project simultaneously without interfering with each other's changes. GitHub provides a user-friendly interface for managing projects, tracking changes, and collaborating through issues, pull requests, and code reviews. It supports both public and private repositories, making it a versatile tool for open-source projects as well as proprietary code. GitHub has become an essential tool for developers worldwide, enabling efficient team collaboration and project management.

Hibernate: An open-source Object-Relational Mapping (ORM) framework for Java applications. It provides a seamless bridge between object-oriented domain models and relational database systems, allowing developers to more efficiently manage and access data. By abstracting the database interactions, Hibernate enables developers to focus on the business logic of their applications, rather than the complexities of SQL queries and database connections. It supports lazy initialization, cache, and various fetching strategies, making data manipulation and retrieval more efficient and straightforward. Hibernate's ability to map Java classes to database tables and automatically generate SQL queries simplifies the persistence layer's development, making it a popular choice for Java-based enterprise applications.

IDE (Integrated Development Environment): A software application that provides comprehensive facilities to programmers for software development, including a code editor, compiler, debugger, and more.

Importing Classes: Bringing in code from different parts of Java or external libraries so you can use their functionalities in your program. Imagine borrowing tools from a toolbox; importing classes lets you borrow and use pre-made code tools, making it easier to add features without writing everything from scratch. This helps keep your code clean and efficient while expanding what your program can do.

Interface: A blueprint for a class. It's a way to outline methods that a class must implement, without specifying how these methods should be carried out. Think of it as a list of promises that a class makes to do certain tasks. Interfaces help ensure that different classes can work together smoothly, even if they perform tasks in different ways.

Inheritance: A feature of object-oriented programming that allows a new class to absorb an existing class's properties and behaviors and enhance them if needed.

Input: The information or data that a program receives. This can come from various sources such as a user typing on a keyboard, a file on the computer, or a sensor in a device. In Java, input helps the program interact with the outside world, allowing it to respond to user commands, read files, or collect data for processing.

Instance Variables: Unique characteristics or properties that belong to each object of a class in Java. Imagine you have a class called "Bike," and each Bike object can have a different color, brand, or speed. These characteristics (color, brand, speed) are instance variables. They help distinguish one object from another, storing data unique to each instance of the class.

JAR (Java ARchive): A package file format used to aggregate many Java class files and associated metadata and resources into one file for distribution.

Java: A high-level, class-based, object-oriented programming language designed to have as few implementation dependencies as possible.

JDK (Java Development Kit): The software development environment used for developing Java applications and applets. It includes the JRE, an interpreter/loader (Java), a compiler (javac), an archiver (jar), a documentation generator (Javadoc), and other tools needed in Java development.

JRE (Java Runtime Environment): Part of the JDK that contains the set of tools for running Java applications, including the JVM.

Jump or Branching Statements: commands that change the usual line-by-line running order of code. They're like choosing different paths based on certain conditions or wanting to skip some steps. The most common ones are `break`, to exit loops; `continue`, to skip to the next loop iteration; and `return`, to exit methods. These statements help control the flow of your program, making it react differently under various conditions or scenarios.

JUnit: An open-source framework used for testing code in the Java programming language. It is a crucial tool in the practice of test-driven development (TDD), providing an efficient way to organize, run, and analyze tests. With JUnit, developers can easily write and keep track of automated unit tests to ensure their code behaves as expected, helping to catch errors early in the development process and maintain high code quality. JUnit is widely used in the Java community due to its simplicity, robustness, and ability to integrate with development environments and build tools.

JVM (Java Virtual Machine): An abstract computing machine that enables a computer to run a Java program. It translates Java bytecode into machine code.

Local Variables: Temporary notes you make while doing a task in Java. They exist only within a specific area, as a function or block of code, and can't be used outside of it. Once you're done with that task or leave that area, those notes disappear. This helps keep things organized and prevents mix-ups with other parts of your program.

Logical Operators: See Operators

Loop: A programming concept that repeats a block of code multiple times. In Java, loops let you run the same code over and over, as if going around a racetrack, until a certain condition is met, such as reaching the finish line. This is especially useful for tasks that need repetition, such as counting numbers, going through items in a list, or performing an action a specific number of times.

Method: A collection of statements grouped together to perform an operation. Methods are defined within a class or object.

Modifier: A keyword in Java that you add to classes, methods, or variables to change their behavior. For example, some modifiers make a method accessible from anywhere in your program, while others restrict access to just within its own class. They help you control how different parts of your program interact, enhancing security and functionality.

NetBeans: An open-source IDE for developing with Java, PHP, C++, and other programming languages.

Object: An instance of a class that includes real-world entities with state and behavior.

Operators: Special symbols that perform specific operations on one, two, or three operands, then return a result. Arithmetic operators are: add (+), subtract (-), multiply (*), or divide (/) numbers. There are different types, including arithmetic for math operations, relational to compare values (< `or` >), logical to work with `true` or `false` conditions, and bitwise with `AND, OR, XOR`. Operators help you manipulate data and make decisions in your code, turning Java into a powerful tool for solving problems. For Ternary operators, see Ternary operators. See Assignment Operators for its definition.

Output: Any information or data that a program sends out. This can be text displayed on the screen, a file that gets created or modified, or even data sent to another device. In Java, commands such as `System.out.println` are used to show output on the screen, helping us see the results of our code's operations or troubleshooting by displaying messages and values.

Package: A folder that organizes and groups together related classes and interfaces. This helps keep your code neatly organized and prevents naming conflicts by allowing you to use the same class name in different packages. Just as you might use folders to organize documents on your computer, packages help manage and structure your Java projects for easy access and maintenance.

Polymorphism: A concept in object-oriented programming that refers to the ability of a variable, function, or object to take on multiple forms.

Prompt Engineering: Teaching ChatGPT how to have a conversation. Prompt engineering involves carefully designing questions and commands that help AI tools such as chatbots understand and respond in a helpful way. It's as if crafting a guidebook so the AI knows the best way to help with coding tasks, answer questions, or follow instructions.

Serialization: The process of converting an object into a format that can be easily stored or transmitted. Imagine taking a picture of a sculpture so you can send it to a friend or store it in an album. Similarly, serialization takes a snapshot of an object's state (its data) and converts it into a byte stream, which can then be saved to a file or sent over a network.

Spring: A comprehensive framework for developing Java applications. It simplifies the creation of complex software by providing infrastructure support at the application level. Spring allows developers to focus on the business logic of their application by handling common tasks such as database interaction, web application development, and security. Its core feature is dependency injection, which promotes loose coupling and easier testing. Spring supports a wide range of application scenarios, from web services and security to accessing data and messaging. Its modular nature means developers can pick and choose which components of Spring they need, making it a versatile choice for building high-performance, robust Java applications.

SQL (Structured Query Language): A standard programming language specifically designed for managing and manipulating relational databases. SQL enables users to perform various tasks such as querying data, updating databases, creating and modifying schemas, and controlling access to the database's data. It works by executing commands that interact with the database's tables and records, allowing for the retrieval, insertion, updating, and deletion of data. Due to its simplicity, efficiency, and widespread support across various database management systems like MySQL, PostgreSQL, SQL Server, and SQLite, SQL is an essential skill for database administrators, data analysts, and software developers working with data-intensive applications.

Static Variables: Shared variables across all instances of a class, meaning they hold the same value for every object of that class. It's like a common locker that all students of a class can access and store shared items. Static variables are great for storing data that needs to be consistent across all objects, such as a count of how many objects have been created from that class.

Streams: Sequences of data. Think of a stream as a water pipe that carries water from one place to another. In Java, streams carry data from a source (a file or network connection) to a destination. They come in two main types: input streams read data into your program, and output streams write data from your program to somewhere else. Streams help your Java programs interact with data smoothly and efficiently.

String: A sequence of characters treated as a single data item and manipulated according to the rules of string processing.

Ternary Operators: a shortcut in Java for making quick decisions. It's as if asking a yes-or-no question and immediately getting a response to act on. This operator checks a condition and chooses one of two outcomes: if the condition is true, it picks the first option; if false, the second. It's written as `condition ? option1 : option2`, streamlining code that otherwise needs an if-else statement.

Variable: A piece of memory that can contain a data value. Variables have associated data types and are used to store information that your Java program can manipulate. Check out local, instance, and static variables.

References

1. Retrieved on March 8, 2024 https://www.oracle.com/mysql/what-is-mysql/#:~:text=MySQL%20is%20the%20world%27s%20most,popular%20database%2C%20behind%20Oracle%20Database.
2. Retrieved on March 5, 2024 https://www.freecodecamp.org/news/my-journey-to-becoming-a-web-developer-from-scratch-without-a-cs-degree-2-years-later-and-what-i-4a7fd2ff5503
3. Retrieved on March 5, 2024 https://codeburst.io/how-i-went-from-mopping-floors-at-a-tanning-salon-to-becoming-a-software-developer-7dc4d2e8d21a
4. Retrieved on December 3, 2023 https://jvns.ca/blog/2015/02/17/how-i-learned-to-program-in-10-years/
5. Retrieved on December 13, 2023 https://www.colbycheeze.com/blog/2015/10/zero-to-developer.html
6. Retrieved on March 3, 2024 https://medium.com/cardinal-solutions/how-to-become-a-front-end-developer-or-any-at-that-686faa8ea9af
7. Retrieved on December 23, 2023 https://learn.saylor.org/mod/book/tool/print/index.php?id=33064&chapterid=13197
8. Retrieved on December 23, 2023 https://en.wikipedia.org/wiki/Java_(programming_language)
9. Retrieved on December 23, 2023 https://www.tiobe.com/tiobe-index/
10. Retrieved on December 23, 2023 https://www.jcp.org/en/home/index
11. Retrieved on December 23, 2023 https://forums.oracle.com/ords/apexds/domain/dev-community
12. Retrieved on March 3, 2024 https://stackoverflow.com/questions/tagged/java
13. Retrieved on March 3, 2024 https://enlyft.com/tech/products/java#:~:text=We%20have%20data%20on%20448%2C975,1M%2D10M%20dollars%20in%20revenue.
14. Retrieved December 28, 2023 https://www.axon.dev/blog/is-java-still-relevant-in-2022#:~:text=Java%20Popularity%20in%202024,-Is%20Java%20still%20relevant%3F
15. Retrieved December 28, 2023 https://www.glassdoor.com/Salaries/java-developer-salary-SRCH_KO0,14.htm
16. Retrieved December 28, 2023 https://www.oracle.com/
17. Retrieved December 28, 2023 https://netbeans.apache.org/

Index

Author Biography

Swift Learning Publications is a pioneering brand at the forefront of technology education, specializing in introducing beginners to the world of Java programming. Born from a collective desire to demystify the complexities of coding for newcomers, Swift Learning Publications stands as a beacon for aspiring developers and tech enthusiasts.

Rooted in a deep commitment to making programming knowledge accessible, Swift Learning Publications has crafted an innovative range of books tailored for those embarking on their coding journey. Our titles span the gamut from introductory Java concepts to more nuanced programming challenges, all designed with the learner in mind.

At Swift Learning Publications, we believe that a strong foundation in Java can unlock a world of opportunities in the tech industry. Our educational materials are curated by a team of seasoned developers and educators who bring real-world experience and pedagogical expertise to every page. Through a blend of practical examples, engaging exercises, and clear, concise explanations, we aim to inspire a new generation of programmers.

Our approach is grounded in the philosophy that learning to code should be an empowering, engaging, and enriching experience. We prioritize clarity, relevance, and practicality, ensuring that every reader can navigate the complexities of Java with confidence and curiosity.

Swift Learning Publications is more than just a brand; it's a community of learners, educators, and innovators. We're on a mission to transform how programming is taught and learned, making it more approachable, enjoyable, and universally accessible. Join us on this exciting journey and unlock the potential of Java programming to shape your future in the technology landscape.

Made in the USA
Middletown, DE
06 April 2025